Quotations
@months and days

AF553408

D Mittal

arihant
ARIHANT PUBLICATIONS (INDIA) LIMITED

ARIHANT PUBLICATIONS (INDIA) LIMITED

卐 **Administrative & Production Offices**

Regd. Office
'Ramchhaya' 4577/15, Agarwal Road, Darya Ganj, New Delhi -110002
Tele: 011- 47630600, 43518550

卐 **Head Office**
Kalindi, TP Nagar, Meerut (UP) - 250002
Tel: 0121-7156203, 7156204

卐 **Sales & Support Offices**
Agra, Ahmedabad, Bengaluru, Bareilly, Chennai, Delhi, Guwahati, Hyderabad, Jaipur, Jhansi, Kolkata, Lucknow, Nagpur & Pune.

卐 **ISBN** 978-93-26197-14-4

卐 **PRICE** ₹150.00

PO No. : TXT-59-T064159-04-25

Published by Arihant Publications (India) Ltd.

For further information about the books published by Arihant, log on to www.arihantbooks.com or e-mail at info@arihantbooks.com

Follow us on  

Contents

Commitment

to live up to

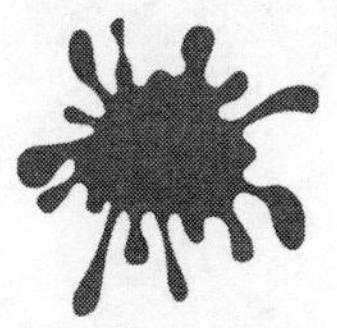

JANUARY 1

- *You must do the thing you think you cannot do.* — Eleaner Roosevelt
- *None but a mule denies his family.* — Moroccan Proverb
- *There are some people that if they don't know, you can't tell them.* — Louis Armstrong
- *Mother are founder than father of their own children because they are more certain they are their own.* — Aristotle
- *The past belongs to us but we do not belong to past, we belong to the present. We are makers of future.* — Mahatma Gandhi
- *I know God will not give me anything I can't handle, I just wish he didn't trust me so much.* — Mother Teresa

JANUARY 2

- *He writes nothing whose writings are not read.* —Martial
- *It is a wise father that knows his own child.* —William Shakespeare
- *The family that prays together stays together.* —Proverb
- *Almost anything you do will be insignificant, but it is very important that you do it.* —Mahatma Gandhi
- *If you steal from one author, it's plagiarism; if you steal from many, it's research.* —Wilson Mizner
- *Is not a patron, my Lord, one who looks with unconcern on a man struggling for life in the water and when he has I reached ground. Encumbers him with help?* —Samuel Johnson

JANUARY 3

- *Fate chooses your relations, you choose your friends.* —Jacques Delille
- *Blood is thicker than water.* —Proverb
- *Men should not care two much for good looks; neglect is becoming.* —Ovid
- *Let reason be opposed to reason and argument to argument, and every good government will be safe.* —Thomas Erskine
- *Poetry is the spontaneous overflow of powerful feelings: it takes its origin from emotion recollected in tranquillity.* —William Wordsworth
- *Poetry should surprise by a fine excess and not by singularity it should strike the reader as a wording of his own highest thoughts, and appear almost a remembrance.* —John Keats

JANUARY 4

- *What men call civilization, always results in deserts.* —Don Marquis
- *A married man with a family will do anything for money.* —Charles De Talleyrand
- *Fear always springs from ignorance.* —Emerson
- *He who sees all beings in his own self and his own self in all beings, loses all fear.* —ISA Upanishad
- *Cowards die many times before their deaths; the valiant never taste of death but once.* —Shakespeare
- *These are the times that try men's souls. The summer soldier and the sunshine patriot will, in this crisis, shrink from the service of their country.* —Thomas Paine

JANUARY 5

- *Civilization is the progress toward a society of privacy.* —Ayn Rand
- *Like father, like son.* —Proverb
- *There's a black sheep in every flock.* —Proverb
- *After a fellow gets famous, it does not take long for someone to bob up that he used to sit by him at school.* —F.M. Hubbard
- *You can't say civilization don't advance ......in every war they kill you in a new way.* —Will Rogers
- *With malice toward none, with charity for all, with firmness in the right, as God gives us to see the right, let us strive on to finish the work we are in, to bind up the nation's wounds.* —Abraham Lincoln

JANUARY 6

- *All quiet along the Potomac.* —George B. Mcclellan
- *A true friend is one soul in two bodies.* —Aristotle
- *I tell you folks, all politics is applesauce.* —Will Rogers
- *The worst friend is he who frequents you in prosperity and deserts you in misfortune.* —Anonymous
- *Satire should, like a polished razor keen, wound with a touch that's scarcely felt or seen.* —Lady Mary Wortley Montagu
- *For a man to write well, there are required three necessaries : to read the best authors, observe the lies! speakers and much exercise of his own style.* —Ben Jonson

JANUARY 7

- *Prosperity makes friends and adversity tries them.* —Anonymous
- *A friend in need is a friend in deed.* —English Proverb
- *All that glitters is not gold.* —Shakespeare
- *Those friends thou hast, and their adoption tried, grapple them to thy soul with hoops to steel.* —Shakespeare
- *If there's a book you really want to read but it hasn't been written yet, then you must write it.* —Toni Morrison
- *The difference between the almost right word and the right word is really a large matter - it's the difference between the lightning bug and the lightning.* —Mark Twain

JANUARY 8

- *The tigers, of wrath are wiser than the horses of instruction.* —William Blake
- *The future is purchased by the present.* —Samuel Johnson
- *Study the past, if you would divine the future.* —Confucius
- *Future is that period of time in which our affairs prosper, our friends are true and our happiness is assured.* —Ambrose Bience
- *Of all those arts in which the wise excel, Nature's chief masterpiece is writing well.* —John Sheffield
- *Reviewers are usually people who would have been poets, historians, biographers, if they could; they have tried their talents at one or the other, and have failed; therefore they turn critic.* —Samuel Taylor Coleridge

JANUARY 9

- *Anger makes dull men witty, but it keeps them poor.* —Elizabeth I
- *Nobody can become perfect by merely ceasing to act.* —Bhagavad Gita
- *Genius does not argue, it creates.* —Rabindranath Tagore
- *I have learned to live each day as it comes and not to borrow trouble by dreading tomorrow.* —Dorothy Dix
- *There's nothing to writing. All you do is sit down at a typewriter and open a vein.* —Walter Red Smith
- *We communists are like seeds and the people are the soil. Wherever we go, we must unite with the people, take root and blossom among them.* —Mao Tse-Tung

JANUARY 10

- *Anger is a brief madness.* —Horace
- *Genius is infinite pains-taking.* —Longfellow
- *Genius must be born, it can never be taught.* —Dryden
- *Drop the question what tomorrow may bring, and count as profit every day that fate allows you.* —Horace
- *A great writer is, so to speak, a second government in his country. And for that reason, no regime has ever loved great writers, only minor ones.* —Alexander Solzhenitsyn
- *I've got a little list -I've got a little list. Of society offenders who might well be underground and who never would be missed-who never would be missed.* —W.S. Gilbert

JANUARY 11

- *Hold the fort! I am coming.* —William Sherman
- *He that is overcautious will accomplish little.* —Schiller
- *What's done can't be undone.* —Shakespeare
- *It is a miserable state of mind to have few things to desire and many things to fear.* —Francis Bacon
- *Writing, when properly managed (as you may be sure I think mine is), is but a different name for conversation.* —Laurence Sterne
- *Any man, might do a girl in*
  any man has to, needs to wants to
  once in a lifetime, do a girl in. —T.S. Eliot

JANUARY 12

- *Buying and selling is essentially antisocial.* —Edward Bellamy
- *Even God cannot change the past.* —Agathon
- *To fulfil God in life is man's manhood.* —Sri Aurobindo
- *Forsake not an old friend; for the new is not comparable to him; a new friend is as new wine.* —Bible
- *A man is a critic when he cannot be an artist, in the same way that a man becomes an informer when he cannot be a soldier.* —Gustave Flaubert
- *You may abuse a tragedy, though you cannot write one. You may scold a carpenter who has made you a bad table, though you cannot make a table. It is not your trade to make tables.* —Samuel Johnson

JANUARY 13

- *What is robbing a bank compared with founding a bank?* —Bertolt Brecht
- *Successful action tends to become an end in itself.* —Erichoffer
- *To do nothing is in every man's power.* —Samuel Johnson
- *Friendship needs no words-it is solltude delivered from the anguish of loneliness.* —Dag Hammarskjold
- *Out of the mouth of babes and sucklings hast thou ordained strength.* —Bible
- *People of the same trade seldom meet together, even for merriment and diversion, but the conversation ends in a conspiracy against the public or in some contrivance to raise prices.* —Adam Smith

JANUARY 14

- *It is better to lose opportunity than capital.* —Susan M. Byrne
- *Art is difficult, transient is her reward.* —Schiller
- *God is one, but He has innumerable forms.* —Guru Nanak
- *One thing is certain and the rest is lies;*
  The flower that once has blown forever dies. —Omar Khayyam
- *All charming people, I fancy, are spoiled. It is the secret of their attraction.* —Oscar Wilde
- *We do not talk-we bludgeon one another with facts and theories gleaned from cursory readings of newspapers, magazines and digests.* —Henry Miller

JANUARY 15

- *Few people do business well who do nothing else.* —Earl of Chesterfield
- *No question is ever settled until it is settled right now.* —Ella Wheeler Wilcox
- *Art is indeed not the bread but the wine of life.* —Jean Paul Richter
- *Flowers are the sweetest things that God ever made and forgot to put a soul into.* —H.W. Beecher
- *All charming people have something to conceal, usually their total dependence on the appreciation of others.* —Cyril Connolly
- *It is my belief, Watson, founded upon my experience, that the lowest and vilest alleys in London do not present a more dreadful record of sin than does the smiling and beautiful countryside.* —A. Conan Doyle

JANUARY 16

- *No nation was ever ruined by trade.* —Benjamin Franklin
- *Arguments out of a petty mouth are unanswerable.* —Joseph Addison
- *Art is like a border of flowers along the course of civilization.* —Lincoln Steffens
- *All happy families resemble one another, each unhappy family is unhappy in its own way.* —Leo Tolstoy
- *Charm is a way of getting the answer yes without ever having asked a clear question.* —Albert Camus
- *I hate doctors! They'll do anything- anything to keep you coming to them. They'll sell their souls! What's worse, they'll sell yours and you never know it till one day you find yourself in hell!* —Eugene Oneill

JANUARY 17

- *Trade is a social act.* —John Stuart Mill
- *Insolence is not logic; epithets are the arguments of malice.* —Ingersoll
- *Art is the lie that enables us to realize the truth.* —Pablo Picasso
- *If you would not be forgotten as soon as you are dead, either write things worth reading or do things worth writing.* —Benjamin Franklin
- *I would rather be attacked than unnoticed. For the worst thing you can do to an author is to be silent as to his work.* —Samuel
- *Recession is when your neighbour loses his job; depression is when you lose yours.*

What we might call, by way of eminence, the dismal science. —Thomas Carlyle

JANUARY 18

- *The customer is always right.* —R Gordon Selfridge
- *Strong and bitter words indicate a weak cause.* —Victor Hugo
- *Art is a faithful mirror of the life and civilization of a period.* —Jawaharlal Nehru
- *Consider the lilies of the field, how they grow; they toil not, neither do they spin.* —Matthew (Bible)
- *Our American professors like their literature clear and cold and pure and very dead.* —Sinclair Lewis
- *Under democracy, one party always devotes its chief efforts to trying to prove that the other is unfit to rule and both commonly succeed and are right.* —H.L. Mencken

JANUARY 19

- *Paris is well worth a mass.* —Henry IV
- *Neither irony nor sarcasm is argument.* —Rufus Choate
- *Art is not an end in itself, but a means of addressing humanity.* —M.P. Moussorgsky
- *Fear is always a feeling to be rejected, because, what you fear is just the thing that is likely to come to you.* —Shri Aurobindo
- *Every suppressed or expunged word reverberates through the earth from side to side.* —Ralph Waldo Emerson
- *Let us rise up and part; she will not know.*
  Let us go seaward as the great winds go,
  full of blown sand and foam. —Algernon Chayes Swinburne

JANUARY 20

- *Childhood is the kingdom where no one dies.* —Edna ST. Vincent Millay
- *Art is the most intense mode of individualism that the world has known.* —Oscar Wilde
- *My poor are my best patients. God pays for them.* —Boerhaave
- *No true and permanent fame can be founded except in labours which promote the happiness of mankind.* —Charles Sumner
- *The trouble with the profit system has always been that it was highly unprofitable to most people.* —E.B. White
- *She had a heart-how shall I say? – too soon made glad,*
  too easily impressed. —Robert Browning

JANUARY 21

- *All art is but imitation of nature.* —Seneca
- *Everyone is the child of his past.* —Edna G. Rostow
- *Art is long and time is fleeting.* —Longfellow
- *It is not death that a man should fear, but he should fear never beginning to live.* —Marcus Aurelius
- *Conspicuous consumption of valuable goods is a means of reputability to the gentleman of leisure.* —Thorstein Veblen
- *Her taste exact for faultless fact*
amounts to a disease. —W.S. Gilbert

JANUARY 22

- *Every baby born into the world is a finer one than the last.* —Charles Dickens
- *The charity in life is more than all ceremonies.* —Talmud
- *Art is not a thing; it is a way.* —Elbert Hubbard
- *Men think highly of those who rise rapidly in the world whereas nothing rises quicker than dust, straw and feathers.* —Hare
- *That which is common to the greatest number has the least care bestowed upon it.* —Aristotle
- *Rejoice with me; for I have found my sheep which was lost ...... joy shall be in heaven over one that repenteth, more than over ninety and nine just persons, which need no repentance.* —Bible

JANUARY 23

- *The childhood shows the man, as morning shows the day.* —Milton
- *A picture is a poem without words.* —Horace
- *A little child shall lead them.* —Bible
- *Fame to the ambitious is like salt water to the thirsty, the more one gets, the more he wants.* —Elbers
- *If poetry comes not as naturally as the leaves to a tree, it had better not come at all.* —IBID
- *The roulette table pays nobody except him who keeps it. Nevertheless a passion for gaming is common, though a passion for keeping roulette wheels is unknown.* —George Bernard Shaw

JANUARY 24

- *The child is father of man.* —Wordsworth
- *Art does not imitate but interprets.* —Mazzini
- *Of all the animals, the boy is the most unmanageable.* —Plato
- *Love of fame is the last thing even learned men can bear to be parted from.* —Tacitus
- *We poets in our youth begin in gladness; but thereof come in the end despondency and madness.* —William Wordsworth
- *The holy passion of friendship is so sweet and steady and loyal and enduring in nature that it will last through a whole lifetime, if not asked to lend money.* —Mark Twain

JANUARY 25

- *Mankind owes to the child the best it has to give.* —U.N. Declaration
- *Art lies in concealing art.* —Ovid
- *Glory to God in the highest and on earth peace, good will toward men.* —IBID
- *Full many a flower is born to blush unseen,*
  and waste its sweetness on the desert air. —Gray
- *You won't, have Nixon to kick around anymore, because,*
  gentlemen, this is my last press conference. —Richard M. Nixon
- *What fools indeed we mortals are to lavish care upon; a car*
  With ne'er bit of time to see about our own machinery. —Anonymous

JANUARY 26

- *"Bah," said Scrooge. "Humbug"!* Charles Dickens
- *Children are our most valuable natural resource.* —Herbert Hoover
- *Nature abhors a vacuum.* —Francois Rabelais
- *And I will make thee beds of roses and a thousand fragrant posies.* —Christopher Marlowe
- *What is a communist? One who hath yearnings for eyuul division of unequal earnings.* —Ebenezer Elliott
- *Like bone to the human body, and the axle to the wheel,*
  and the song to a bird, and air to the wing, thus is liberty
  the essence of life. Whatever is done without it is imperfect. —Jose Marti

JANUARY 27

- *"God bless us everyone!" said Tiny Tim, the last of all.* —IBID
- *One touch of nature makes the whole world kin.* —Shakespeare
- *Everything in nature acts in conformity with law.* —Immanuel Kant
- *A conservative is a man with two perfectly good legs who, however, has never learned how to walk forward.* —IBID
- *From Stettin in the Baltic to Trieste in the Adriatic, an iron curtain has descended across the Continent.* —Winston Churchill
- *I had reasoned this out in my mind : There was two things I had a right to liberty and death. If I could not have one, I would have the other, for no man should take me alive.*

  —Harriet Tubman

JANUARY 28

- *Books are for nothing but to inspire.* —Ralph Waldo Emerson
- *From labour health; from health contentment springs.* —Anonymous
- *Fear is the mother of morality.* —Friedrich Neitzsche
- *Flowers are words which even a babe may understand.* —Bishop Coxe
- *An inveterate and incurable itch for writing besets many and grows old with their sick hearts.* —Juvenal
- *Civilisation advances by extending the number of important operations which we can perform without thinking about them.*

  —Alfred North Whitehead

JANUARY 29

- *Nature admits no lie.* —Thomas Carlyle
- *Fear is the foundation of safety.* —Tertullia
- *Read in order to live.* —Gustave Flaubert
- *Fame is like a river, that beareth up things light and swollen, and drowns things weighty and solid.* —Francis Bacon
- *Reading all the good books is like a conversation with the finest men of past centuries.* —Rene Descartes
- *All good books are alike in that they are truer than if they really happened and after you are finished reading one you will feel that it all happened to you, and afterwards it all belongs to you.* —Ernest Hemingway

JANUARY 30

- *It could not have been foreseen by any logical process.* —Sir Kenneth Clark
- *Nature is commanded by obeying her.* —Francis Bacon
- *Laugh and grow fat.* —Proverb
- *Never does the human soul appear so strong as when it forgoes revenge, and dares forgive an injury.* —E.H. Chapin
- *The forces of a capitalist society, if left unchecked, tend to make the rich richer and the poor poorer.* —Jawaharlal Nehru
- *Happiness is an imaginary condition formerly often attributed by the living to the dead, now usually attributed by adults to children, and by children to adults.* —Thomas Szasz

JANUARY 31

- *Extraordinary how potent cheap music is.* —Noel Coward
- *Nature has always had more force than education.* —Vathaire
- *For Art may err, but nature cannot miss.* —Dryden
- *I awoke one morning and found myself famous.* —Byron
- *I disapprove of what you say,*
  but I will defend to the death your right to say it. —Voltaire
- *Fearlessness should never mean want of due respect*
  or regard for the feelings of others. —M.K. Gandhi
- *What is good for the country is good for General Motors,*
  and what is good for General Motors is good for the country.
  —Charles. E. Wilson
- *I believe it is peace for our time.* —Neville Chamberlain
- *The journey of a thousand miles, begins with one step.* —Lao Tzu
- *When power narrows the areas of man's concern,*
  poetry remains him of the richness and diversity
  of his existence. When power corrupts, poetry cleanses. —John F. Kennedy
- *There was a time when corporations played a minor part*
  in our business affairs, but know they play the chief part,
  and most men are the servants of corporations. —Woodrow Wilson
- *We don't know that we don't know.* —Unknown
- *If you don't decide which way to play with life,*
  it always play with you. —Merle Shain
- *The artist who aims at perfection in everything*
  achieves nothing. —Eugene Delacroix

Innovation

beyond expectation

FEBRUARY 1

- *What passion cannot, music raise and quell?* —John Dryden
- *Lack of money is the root of all evil.* —George Bernard Shaw
- *Adopt the pace of nature, her secret is patience.* —R.W. Emerson
- *Without forgiveness life is governed by ...... an endless cycle of resentment and retaliation.* —Roberto Assagioli
- *Laissez Faire.*
  Let business go forward. No interference. —Marquis D' Argenson
- *Happiness is the only sanction in life; where happiness fails, existence remains a mad and lamentable experiment.* —George Santayana

FEBRUARY 2

- *Hold as 'twere the mirror up to nature.* —IBID
- *Money is a good servant but a bad master.* —Francis Bacon
- *Nature is a volume of which God is the author.* —Harvey
- *Look upon all the annihilate beings as your bosom friends, for in all of them there resides one soul.* —Rig Veda
- *Books are good enough in their own way but they are a mighty bloodless substitute for life.*
  —Robert Louis Stevenson

FEBRUARY 3

- *Civilization is a race between education and catastrophe.* —H.G. Wells
- *Fear was the first thing on earth to make Gods.* —Lucretius
- *Exit, pursued by a bear.* —Shakespeare
- *Painting is the art of protecting flat surfaces from the weather and exposing them to the critic.* —Ambrose Bierce
- *A market is a place set apart for men to deceive-and get the better of-one another.* —Anacharsis

FEBRUARY 4

- *A good critic is one who describes his adventures among masterpieces.* —Anatole France
- *Everyone is innocent until he is proved guilty.* —Proverb
- *Law-makers should not be law-breakers.* —Proverb
- *A flattering painter who made it his care to draw men as they ought to be, not as they are.* —Goldsmith
- *Corporations nave neither bodies to be punished, nor souls to be condemned, they therefore do as they like.* —Edward, First Baron Thurlow
- *As good almost kill a man as kill a good book: who kills a man kills a reasonable creature, God's image; but he who destroys a good book, kills reason itself.* —John Milton

FEBRUARY 5

- *All children are essentially criminal.* —Denis Diderot
- *No sweat, no sweet.* —Proverb
- *I cannot live without books.* —Thomas Jefferson
- *Most people see by way of their parents, their masters, or the social milieu in which they live.* —Germain Bazin
- *They (corporations) cannot commit treason, nor be outlawed, nor excommunicate, for they have no souls.* —Edward Coke
- *We hold these truths to be self-evident; that all men are created equal; that they are endowed by their creator with certain unalienable rights; that among these are life, liberty and the pursuit of happiness.* —Thomas Jefferson

FEBRUARY 6

- *Be you ever so high, the law is above you.* —Thomas Fuller
- *Civilization-the victory of persuasion over force.* —Palmer Wright
- *We shouldn't teach great books; we should teach a love of reading.* —B.F. Skinner
- *I believe the greatest asset a head of state can have is the ability to get a good night's sleep.* Harold Wilson
- *There is no such thing as a moral or an immoral book. Books are well written or badly written.* —Oscar Wilde
- *Our manifest destiny is to overspread the continent allotted by Providence for the free development of our yearly multiplying millions.* —John L. O' Sullivan

FEBRUARY 7

- *History, a distillation of rumor.* —Thomas Carlyle
- *Petty laws breed great crimes.* —Ouida
- *People say that life is the thing, but I prefer reading.* —Logan Pearsall Smith
- *The connoisseur of painting gives only bad advice to the painter. For that reason I have given up trying to judge myself.* —Pablo Picasso
- *A good book is the best of friends, the same today and forever.* —Martin F. Tupper
- *For we must consider that we shall be a city upon a hill.*
- *You shall not press down upon the brow of labor this crown of thorns. You shall not crucify mankind upon a cross of gold.* —William Jennings Bryan

FEBRUARY 8

- *Bad laws are the worst sort of tyranny.* —Edmund Burke
- *All things are artificial, for nature is the art of God.* —Thomas Browne
- *Literature... becomes the living memory of a nation.* —Alexander Solzhenitsyn
- *The past must no longer be used as an anvil for beating out the present and the future.* —Paul-Emile Bolduas
- *Books are the treasured wealth of the world and the fit inheritance of generations and nations.* —Thoreau
- *It is not from the benevolence of the butcher, the brewer or the baker that we expect our dinner, but from their regard to their own self-interest.* —IBID

FEBRUARY 9

- *Nature does nothing in vain.* —Proverb
- *No man ever yet became great by imitation.* —Samuel Johnson
- *Reading is to the mind what exercise is to the body.* —Richard Steele
- *Science has achieved more for the emancipation of masses than the wisdom of sages.* —S. Radhakrishnan
- *How many a man has dated a new era in his life from the rending of a book.* —IBID
- *Scenes of passion should not be introduced when not essential to the plot. In general, passion should be so treated that these scenes do not stimulate the lower and baser element.* —The Motion Picture Producers and Distributors

FEBRUARY 10

- *Literature is my utopia.* —Hlen Keller
- *Labour is life.* —Thomas Carlyle
- *Laughter is the best medicine.* —Proverb
- *Only work, which is the product of inner compulsion can have spiritual meuning.* —Walter Gropius
- *Whenever I hear-the word "culture,"... I release the safety catch on my Browning!* —Hanns Johst
- *Welcome O life! I go to encounter for the millionth time the reality of experience and to forge in the smithy of my soul the uncreated conscience of my race.* —James Joyce

FEBRUARY 11

- *Human history is in essence a history of ideas.* —H.G. Wells
- *Virtue is the first title of nobility.* —J.B. Moliere
- *I cried all the way to the bank (response to negative reviews).* —Liberace
- *This is such a serious world that we should never speak at all unless we have something to say.* —Thomas Carlyle
- *Mrs. Ballinger is one of the ladies who pursue culture in bands, as though it were dangerous to meet it alone.* —Edith Wharton
- *I had reasoned this out in my mind; There was two things had a right to, liberty and death. If I could not have one, would have the-other, for no man should take me alive.* —Harriet Tubman

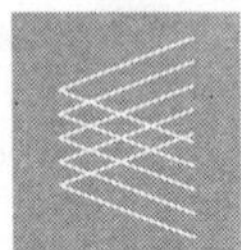

FEBRUARY 12

- *Riches either serve or govern the possessor.* —Horqce
- *War is death's feast.* —Proverb
- *Nor in the critic let the man be lost.* —Alexander Pope
- *If people only knew as much about my painting as I do, they would never buy my pictures.* —Edwin Landseer
- *The true artist will let his wife starve, his children go barefoot, his mother drudge for his living at seventy, sooner than work at anything but his art.* —George Bernard Shaw
- *Like bone to the human body, and the axle to the wheel, and the song to a bird, and air to the wing, thus is liberty the essence of life. Whatever is done without it is imperfect.* —Jose Marti

FEBRUARY 13

- *A picture is a poem without words.* —Horace
- *In a war of ideas, it is people who get killed.* —S.I.Lec
- *O! for a Muse of fire, that would ascend the brightest heaven of invention!* —Shakespeare
- *Interpretation is the revenge of the intellect upon art.* —Susan Sontag
- *Silence is as full of potential wisdom and wit as the unheaven marble of great sculpture.* —Aldous Huxley
- *I am all that has been, and that is, and that shall remain, and no one unworthy has ever unraveled, loosened or even touched the surface of my woven veil.* —Anonymous

FEBRUARY 14

- *Even God cannot change the past.* —Aristotle
- *Painted pictures are dead speakers.* —Proverb
- *Never meddle with play actors, for they're favored race.* —Cervantes
- *O sleep, O gentle sleep nature's soft nurse.* —Shakespeare
- *Music is the universal language of mankind-poetry their universal pastime and delight.* —Henry Wadsworth Longfellow
- *Happiness is an imaginary condition formerly often attributed by the living to the dead, now usually attributed by adults to children, and by children to adults.* —Thomas Szasz

FEBRUARY 15

- *If a gun is hanging on the wall in the first act, it must fire in the last.* —Anton Chekhov
- *Adopt the pace of nature; her secret is patience.* —R.W. Emerson
- *He that can have patience can have what he will.* —Franklin
- *The past can never be effaced, since the recollection of it is an element in shaping the future.* —James Bryce
- *A falseness in all our impressions of external things, which I would generally characterize as the "pathetic fallacy".* —John Ruskin
- *There are two things to aim at in life; first, to get what you want; and, after that, to enjoy it. Only the wisest of mankind achieve the second.* —Logan Pearsall Smith

FEBRUARY 16

- *Satire is what close on Saturday night.* —George S.Kaufman
- *There is no gambling like politics.* —Disraeli
- *Wars bring scars.* —English Proverb
- *The windows of my soul I throw wide open to the sun.* —Whittier
- *Wherever they burn books, they will also i n the end, burn people.* —Heinrich Heine
- *Government is a contrivance of human wisdom to provide for human wants. Men have a right that these wants should be provided for by this wisdom.* —Edmund Burke

FEBRUARY 17

- *No good man ever became suddenly rich.* —Syrus
- *Virtue and happiness are mother and daughter.* —Proverb
- *Drama is action, sir, action and no; confounded philosophy.* —Luigi Pirandello
- *The restless swan-the human soul-is on the journey infinite to find out the truth.* —Rig Veda
- *Music, the greatest good that mortals know, and all of heaven we have here below.* —Joseph Addison
- *The way of an eagle in the air; the way of a serpent upon a rock; the way of a ship in the midst of the sea; and the way of a man with a maid.* —IBID

FEBRUARY 18

- *I call architecture frozen music.* —Goethe
- *Pictures must not be too picturesque.* —R.W. Emerson
- *Beware the fury of a patient man.* —Dryden
- *How wonderful is Death, death and his brother Sleep!* —Shelley
- *Whether angles play only Bach in praising God, I am not sure. I am sure, however, that en famille they play Mozart.* —Karl Barth
- *For unto everyone that hath shall be given, and he shall have abundance; but from him that hath not shall be taken even that which he hath.* —Bible

FEBRUARY 19

- *All wealth is the product of labour.* —Locke
- *Politics is a blood sport.* —Aneurin Bevan
- *One might regard architecture as history arrested in stone.* —A. L. Rowse
- *What sight is sadder than the sight of a lady we admire admiring a nauseating picture?* —Logan Pearsall Smith
- *Suit the action to the word, the word to the action, with this special observance, that you overstep not the modesty of nature.* —IBID
- *Cruelty has a human heart,*
  and jealousy a human face;
  Terror, the human form divine,
  and Secrecy, the human dress. —William Blake

FEBRUARY 20

- *When we build let us think that we build forever.* —John Ruskin
- *Not heaven itself upon the past has power.* —Dryden
- *Every war is a national misfortune.* —Helmuth Von Moltke
- *It is a great misfortune neither to have enough wit to talk well nor enough judgement to be silent.* —La Bruyere
- *The play's the thing*
  wherein I'll catch the conscience of the king. —Shakespeare
- *That which does not kill us makes us stronger.* —Friedrich Nietzsche

FEBRUARY 21

- *The best prophet of the future is the past.* —John Sherman
- *I tell you the past is a bucket of ashes.* —Carl Sandburg
- *Pleasure is by no means an infallible guide but it is the least fallible.* —W.H. Auden
- *Blessed are they who have nothing to say,*
  and who cannot be persuaded to say it. —Lowell
- *Speak the speech, I pray you, as I pronounced it to you,*
  trippingly on the tongue. —IBID
- *His life was gentle and the elements*
  so mixed in him that Nature might stand up
  and say to all the world, "This was a man". —IBID

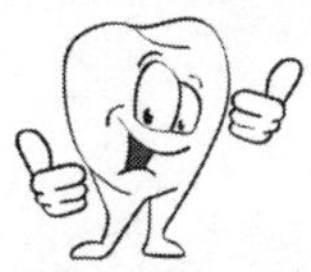

FEBRUARY 22

- *They also serve who only stand and wait.* —Milton
- *Great artists have no country.* —Alfred De Musset
- *Patience is the art of hoping.* —Vauvenargues
- *Science has promised us truth. It has never promised us either peace or happiness.* —Custave Le Bon
- *Chicago is the product of modern capitalism and*
  like other great commercial centers is unfit for human habitation. —Eugene Debs
- *If you are lucky enough to have lived in Paris*
  as a young man then wherever you go for the rest
  of your life, it stays with you. For Paris is a moveable feast. —Ernest Hemingway

FEBRUARY 23

- *Less is more.* —Ludwig Mies Van Der Rohe
- *Poverty is not a crime.* —Proverb
- *The past at least is secure.* —Daniel Webster
- *A little philosophy inclineth man's mind to atheism; but depth in philosophy bringeth men's minds about to religion.* —Francis Bacon
- *Go out into the highways and hedges and compel them to come in, that my house may be filled.* —Bible
- *Use your health, even to the point of wearing it out. That is what it is for. Spend all you have before you die; and do not Outlive yourself.* —George Bernard Shaw

FEBRUARY 24

- *Our patience will achieve more than our force.* —Edmund Burke
- *Though patience be a tired mare, yet she will plod.* —William Shakespeare
- *Poverty partite fellowship.* —Proverb
- *You will never have a quiet world till you knock patriotism out of the human race.* —George Bernard Shaw
- *Only through art can we emerge from ourselves and know what another person sees.* —Marcel Proust
- *But at my back I always hear*
  times winged chariot hurrying near;
  And yonder all before us lie
  deserts of vast eternity. —IBID

FEBRUARY 25

- *We must learn to walk before we can run.* —Proverb
- *Patience and passage of time do more than strength and fury.* —Jean De La Fontaine
- *All art is but imitation of nature.* —Seneca
- *There are more things in heaven and earth, Horatio, than are dreamt of in your philosophy.* —Shakespeare
- *To establish oneself in the world, one has to do all one can to appear established.* —La Rochefoucauld
- *To make much of time had we but world enough and time, this coyness, Lady, were no crime.* —Andrew Marvell

FEBRUARY 26

- *All art is quite useless.* —Oscar Wilde
- *Poverty is the test of civility and the touchstone of friendship.* —Hazlitf
- *Rome was not built in a day.* —Proverb
- *The world is my country, all mankind are my brethren, and to do good is my religion.* —Thomas Paine
- *Speak when you are angry and you will make the best speech you will ever regret.* —Ambrose Bierce
- *In him was life; and the life was the light of men. And the light shineth in darkness; and the darkness comprehended it not.* —IBID

FEBRUARY 27

- *Patience is a minor form of despair, disguised as a virtue.*
—Ambrose Bierc
- *God cannot alter the past but historians can.* —Samuel Butler
- *Form ever follows function.* —Louis Henri Sullivan
- *Poetry is the record of the best and happiest*
moments of the happiest and best minds. —Shelley
- *Common-looking people are the best in the world; that is the reason the Lord makes so many of them.* —Abraham Lincoln
- *A judge is not supposed to know anything about the facts of*
life until they have been presented into evidence and explained to him at least three times. —Lord Chief Justice Parker

FEBRUARY 28

- *Architecture is inhabited sculpture.* —Brancusi
- *The best friend one can have is the past.* —Baroness De Krudener
- *Everything comes to him who waits.* —Proverb
- *The more you read about politics, you get to admit*
that each party is worse than the other. —Will Rogers
- *Hell is a city much like London*
a populous and smoky city. —Percy Bysshe Shelley
- *Now hast thou but one bare hour to live*
and then thou must be damned perpetually!
Stand still you ever-moving spheres of heaven,
that time may cease and midnight never come.
—Christopher Marlowe

FEBRUARY 29

- *Blessed are those that nought expect,*
  for they shall not be disappointed.
  —Disraelia Symphony is no Joke. Johannes Brahms
- *A still tongue makes a wise head.* —Proverb
- *One merit of poetry few person will deny :*
  It says more and in fewer words than prose. —Voltaire
- *It is our true policy to steer clear of permanent alliances*
  with only portion of the foreign world. —George Washington
- *I have drunken deep of joy,*
  and I will taste no other wine tonight. —Shelley
- *And the Word was made flesh, and dwelt among*
  us (and we beheld his glory, the glory as of the only
  begotten of the Father), full of grace and truth. —IBID
- *Man loves little and often, women much and rarely.* —Basta
- *Everything comes if a man will only wait.* —Disraeli
- *Silence is the most perfect expression of scorn.* —George Bernard Shaw
- *"We trust, sir, that God is one our side."*
  "It is more important to know that we are on God's side."
  —Lincoln During Civil War
- *Strange how much you've got to know.*
  Before you know how little you know. —Anonymous
- *Lord! I wonder what fool it was that first invented kissing.* —Swift
- *Logic is neither a science nor an art, but a dodge.* —Benjamin Jowett
- *Children have more need of models than of critics.* —Joubert

Creativity

to last

MARCH 1

- *The cruelest lies are often told in silence.* —R. L. Stevenson
- *Even victors are by victory undone.* —John Dryden
- *The heart of the melody can never be put down on paper.* —Pablo Casals
- *Politics is perhaps the only profession for which no preparation is thought necessary.* —Robert Louis Stevenson
- *A man who is good enough to shed his blood for his country is good enough to be given a square deal afterward.*

  —Theodore Roosevelt
- *For God so loveth the world, that he gave his only begotten son, that whosoever believeth in him should not perish, but have everlasting life.*

  —IBID

MARCH 2

- *Where there's music, there can be no evil.* —Cervantes
- *Silence is the unbearable repartee.* —Chesterton
- *Without victory there is no survival!* —Winston Churchill
- *Swim or sink, live or die, survive or perish with my country has been my unalterable determination.*

  —John Adams
- *The city is of night; perchance of death, but certainly of night .*

  —James Thomson
- *Ignorance of the law excuses no man; not that all men know the law, but because 'tis an excuse every man will plead, and no man can tell how to refute him.* —John Selden

MARCH 3

- *I'm not a crook.* —Richard M. Nixon
- *He hears but half who hears one party only.* —Aeschylus
- *Prejudice is the child of ignorance.* —Hazlitt
- *Be not slow to visit the sick.* —Ecclesiastes
- *But the tender grace of a day that is dead*
  will never come back to me. —Tennyson
- *To some generations much is given. Of others much is expected.*
  This generation of Americans has a rendezvous with destiny.
  —Franklin D. Roosevelt

MARCH 4

- *They also serve who only stand and wait.* —John Milton
- *I shall return.* —Douglas Macarthur
- *Prejudice is an opinion without judgement.* —Voltaire
- *A fox should not be of the jury at a goose's trial.* —Thomas Fuller
- *If you wish the sympathy of broad masses,*
  then you must tell them the crudest and most stupid things.
  —Adolf Hitler
- *Poetry does not necessarily have to be beautiful*
  to stick in the depths of our memory. —Colfite
- *There are only two or three human stories,*
  and they go on repeating themselves as fiercely
  as if they had never happened before. —Willa Cather

MARCH 5

- *Damn the torpedoes! Full speed ahead.* —David Farragut
- *Patience is a bitter plant but it has sweet fruit.* —German Proverb
- *Only the past is immortal.* —Delmore Schwartz
- *There was never yet a philosopher that could endure the toothache patiently.* —Shakespeare
- *All poets are mad. Genuine poetry can communicate before it is understood.* —T.S. Eliot
- *And here we are as on a darkling plain swept with confused alarms of struggle and flight, where ignorant armies clash by night.* —Mathew Arnold

MARCH 6

- *A man without patience is a lamp without oil.* —Andres Segovia
- *Praise the Lord and pass the ammunition.* —Howell M. Forgy
- *The greatest man in history was the poorest.* —R.W. Emerson
- *Speech is silver, silence is golden.* —German Proverb
- *The bud may have a bitter taste, but sweet will be the flower.* —William Cowper
- *The three great elements of modern civilization - Gunpowder, printing, and the protestant religion.* —Thomas Carlyle
- *There is always inequity in life. Some men are killed in a war and some men are wounded, and some men never leave the country .... life is unfair.* —John F. Kennedy

MARCH 7

- *The world must be made safe for democracy.* —Woodrow Wilson
- *Blessed be ye poor, for yours is the kingdom of God.* —New Testament
- *Poverty makes a man acquainted with strange bed-fellows.* —Proverb
- *The tree is known by his fruit.* —Matthew
- *A politician is an animal who can sit on a fence and yet keep both ears to the ground.* —Anonymous
- *Civilized men arrive in the pacific, armed with alcohol, syphilis, trousers, and the Bible.* —Havelock Ellis
- *I have air my life long been lying (in bed) till noon; yet I tell all young men, and tell them with great sincerity, that no body who does not rise early will ever do any good.* —Samuel Johnson

MARCH 8

- *Poverty is no vice, but an inconvenience.* —John Florio
- *Better a lean peace than a fat victory.* —Proverb
- *Whosoever shall say, Thou fool, shall be in danger of hell fire.* —Bible
- *Pleasure must first have the warrant that it is without sin, then the measure, that it is without excess.* —Henry Gardiner Adams
- *How few our real wants, And how vast our imaginary ones!* —Laveter
- *We think our civilisation near "its meridian, but we are yet only at the cock-crowing and the morning star.* —Ralph Waldo Emerson
- *Iron rusts from disuse, stagnant water loses its purity and in cold weather becomes frozen; even so does inaction sap the vigors of the mind.* —Leonardo Da Vinci

MARCH 9

- *Be ye angry and sin not; let not the sun go down upon your wrath.* —*Bible*
- *Be more eager for truth than for success.* —*The Mother*
- *Success is the sole earthly judge of right and wrong.* —*Hitler*
- *Patience is the virtue of an ass, that trots beneath his burthen, and is quiet.* —*George Granville*
- *Ah, but a man's reach should exceed his grasp, or what's a heaven for?* —*Robert Browning*
- *Laws are like spiders' webs; If some poor weak creature come up against them, it is caught; but a big one can break through and get away.* —*Solon*

MARCH 10

- *Every and wrath shorten the fife.* —*Bible*
- *Poverty is the mother of all arts and trades.* —*Proverb*
- *Science surpasses the old miracles of mythology.* —*R.W. Emerson*
- *Poetry is the music of thought, conveyed to us through the music of language.* —*Chatfield*
- *Children inherit the qualities of the parents, no less than their physical features.* —*M.K. Gandhi*
- *Four score and seven years ago our fathers brought forth on this continent, a new nation conceived in Liberty, and dedicated to the proposition that all men are created equal.* —*Abraham Lincoln*

MARCH 11

- *When angry, count four; when very angry, swear.* —Mark Twain
- *Poverty breeds strife.* —Proverb
- *Success is a public affair, failure is a private funeral.* —Russell
- *Poetry is the sister of sorrow; every man that suffers and weeps is a poet; every tear is a verse; and every heart is a poem.* —Andre
- *Give me your tired, your poor,*
  your huddled masses yearning to breathe free. —Emma Lazarus

MARCH 12

- *Anger supplies the arms.* —Virgil
- *In war there is no substitute for victory.* —Douglas Macarthur
- *Time is precious, but truth is more precious than time.* —Disraeli
- *How poor are they that have not patience!*
  What wound did ever heal but by degrees? —Shakespeare
- *I fear the Greeks, even when they bring gifts.* —Vergil
- *Peace, commerce and honest friendship with all nations*
  entangling alliances with none. —Thomas Jefferson
- *Goodnight! goodnight!*
  Parting is such sweet sorrow
  that I shall say goodnight till it be morrow. —IBID

MARCH 13

- *Appearances are often deceiving.* —Aesop
- *To teach is to learn twice.* —Joseph Jonbert
- *To know how to suggest is the art of teaching.* —Amiel
- *Loyalty must arise spontaneously from the hearts of people who love their country and respect their government.* —Hugo L. Black
- *We must, indeed, all hang together or most assuredly, we shall all hang separately.* —Benjamin Franklin
- *O Romeo, Romeo, where fore art thou Romeo?*
  Deny thy father and refuse thy name,
  Or if thou wilt not, be but sworn my love
  and I'll no longer be a capulet. —IBID

MARCH 14

- *Science is organised knowledge.* —H. Spencer
- *Truth is the first casualty in war.* —Proverb
- *In everything that can be called art there is a quality of redemption.* —Raymond Chandler
- *Keep off your thoughts from things that are past and done; for thinking of the past wakes regret and paln.* – Arthur Waley
- *Well, I think we ought to let him hang there. Let him twist slowly, slowly in the wind.* —John Ehrlichman
- *In the councils of government, we must guard against the acquisition of unwarranted influence, whether sought or unsought, by the military-industrial complex.* —Dwight D. Eisenhower

MARCH 15

- *An artist will betray himself by some sort of sincerity.* —G.K. Chesterton
- *Poverty and wealth are comparative sins.* —Victor Hugo
- *Men are born to succeed, not to fail.* —Hemy David Thoureau
- *Poetry is the spontaneous overflow of powerful feelings .. recollected in tranquillity.* —William Wordsworth
- *Here once the embattled farmers stood,*
  and fired the shot heard round the world.
  —Ralph Wawo Emerson
- *A book of verses underneath the bough*
  a jug of wine, a loaf of bread and thou
  beside me singing in the wilderness. —Edward Fitzgerald

MARCH 16

- *You cannot teach old dogs new tricks.* —Anonymous
- *Science commits suicide, when it adopts a creed.* —Huxley
- *Art is a jealous mistress.* —Ralph W Aldoemerson
- *Hell is paved with good intentions.* —St. Bernard
- *Patriotism is as fierce as a fever, pitiless as the grave,*
  blind as a stone and irrational as a headless hen. —Ambrose Bierce
- *I would remind you that extremism in the defense of liberty is no vice.*
  And let me remind you also that moderation in
  the pursuit of justice is no virtue! —Barry Goldwater
- *There can be no peace of mind in love since the*
  advantage one has secured is never anything but
  a fresh starting point for further desire. —Proust

MARCH 17

- *Art without life is a pool affair.* —Henry James
- *The secret of success is constancy of purpose.* —Disraeli
- *The key to everything is patience. You get the chicken by hatching the egg, not by smashing it.* – Arnold Glasow
- *I know of no country, indeed, where the love of money has taken a stronger hold on the affections of men.* —Alexis De Tocqueville
- *See how she leans her cheek upon her hand! Oh, that I were! a glove upon that hand, that I might touch that cheek!* —William Shakespeare

MARCH 18

- *Success treads on every right step.* —R.W. Emerson
- *Patience is a virtue.* —Proverb
- *The next Augustan age will dawn on the other side of the Atlantic.* —Horace Walpole
- *With malice towards none, with charity for all ...... let us finish the work we are in, to bind up the nation's wounds.* —Abraham Lincoln
- *There can be no fifty-fifty Americanism in this country. There is room here for only hundred percent Americanism.* —Theodore Roosevelt
- *I have found it impossible to carry the heavy burden of responsibility and to discharge my duties as king as I would wish without the help and support of the woman I love.* —Edward

MARCH 19

- *The Constitution does not provide for first and second class citizens.*
  —Wendell Willkie
- *Have no friends not equal to yourself.* —Confucius
- *A friend-may well be reckoned the masterpiece of nature.*
  —Ralph Waldo Emerson
- *Patience is something you admire in the driver*
  behind you and scorn in the one ahead. —M. Mccleary
- *He had a broad face and a little round belly,*
  that shook when he laughed like a bowlful of jelly. —IBID
- *Heap on more wood! the wind is chill,*
  but let it whistle as it will,
  we'll keep our Christmas merry still. —Sir Walter Scott

MARCH 20

- *The future struggles against being mastered.* —Latin Proverb
- *The ripest peach is highest on the tree.* —James Whitcomb Riley
- *A good life is the only religion.* —Thomas Fuller
- *It is not often that someone comes along*
  who is a true friend and good writer. —E. B. White
- *But heard him exclaim, ere he drove out of sight,*
  "Happy Christmas to all and to all a good night!" —IBID
- *Come live with me, and be my love,*
  and we will some new pleasures prove
  of golden sands, and crystal brooks,
  with silken lines, and silver hooks. —John Donne

MARCH 21

- *The essential American soul is hard, isolate, stoics, a killer.*

  —D.H. Lawrence
- *Prayer needs no speech.* —M.K. Gandhi
- *The place of reuson is higher than the place of heart.* —Rig Veda
- *Forsake not an old friend; for the new is not comparable to him; a new friend is as new wine.* —Bible
- *A good novel tells us the truth about its hero; but a bad novel tells us the truth about its author.*

  —G. K. Chesterjqn
- *These I have loved:*
  white plates and cups, clean-gleaming,
  ringed with blue lines. —Rupert Brooke

MARCH 22

- *Ambition should be made of sterner stuff.* —Shakespeare
- *Reading maketh a full man.* —Francis Bacon
- *Poetry is the first and last of all knowledge; it is as immortal as the heart of man.* —William Wordsworth
- *The only thing that can save the world is the reclaiming of the awareness of the world. That's what poetry does.*

  —Allen Ginsberg
- *I love thee with the breath,*
  smiles, tears, of all my life and if God choose,
  I shall but love thee better after death. —IBID
- *The circumstances of others seem good to us while ours seem good to others.* —Syrus

MARCH 23

- *In America, public opinion is the leader.* —Frances Perkins
- *Every why hath a wherefore.* —Shakespeare
- *Religion is nothing else but love to God and man.* —William Penn
- *He that hath no cross deserves no crown.* —Quarels
- *A true friend is the most precious of an possessions and the one we take the least thought about acquiring.* —La Rochefoucauld
- *It is only shallow people who do not judge by appearances. The true mystery of the world is the visible not the invisible.* —Oscar Wilde
- *I was a child and she was a child,*
  in this kingdom by the sea;
  but we loved with a love that was more than love
  I and my Annabel Lee. —Edgar Allan Poe

MARCH 24

- *You cannot conquer America.* —William Pitt
- *I am free of all prejudices. I hate everyone equally.* —W.C. Fields
- *Prayer changes things by changing people.* —Ernest G. Sangster
- *If I had to choose between betraying my country and betraying my friend, I hope I should have the guts to betray my country.* —E.M. Forster
- *There is a price which is too great to pay for peace, and that price can be put in one word. One cannot pay the price of self-respect.* —Woodrow Wilson
- *How many loved your moments of gland grace,*
  and loved your beauty with love false or true;
  but one man loved the pilgrim soul in you,
  and loved the sorrows of your changing face. —IBID

MARCH 25

- *We must be the great arsenal of democracy.* —Franklin D. Roosevelt
- *Religion is behaviour and not mere belief.* —S. Radhakrishnan
- *The best religion is the most tolerant.* —MME De Girarffin
- *What's done can't be undone.* —Shakespeare
- *Friendship needs no words - it is solitude delivered from the anguish of loneliness.* —Dag HammarskJold
- *Better that we should die fighting than be outraged and dishonored...... Better to die than to live in slavery.* —Emmeline Pankhurst
- *When you are old and gray and full of sleep*
  and nodding by the fire, take down this book
  and slowly read. —William Butler Yeats

MARCH 26

- *Strong reasons make strong actions.* —Shakespeare
- *Religion is the opium of people.* —Karl Marx
- *Americans are suckers for good news.* —Adlai Stevenson
- *If a man does not make new acquaintances as he advances through life, he will soon find himself left alone.* —Samuel Johnson
- *If once you have paid him the Dane-geld you never get rid of the Dane.* —Rudyard Kipling
- *Nothing in the world is single; all things by a law divine in one spirit meet and mingle.*
- *Why not I with thine?* —Percy Bysshe Shelley

MARCH 27

- *Reading is to the mind, what exercise is to the body.* —Addison
- *Reason can, in general, do more than blind force.* —Gallis
- *We have met the enemy, and they are ours.* —Oliver Perry
- *Out of the quarrel with others we make rhetoric;*
  out of the quarrel with ourselves we make poetry. —W.B. Yeats
- *The name of peace is sweet and the thing itself is good,*
  but between peace and slavery there is the greatest difference.
  —Cicero
- *A gentleman who had been very unhappy in marriage,*
  married immediately after his wife died; Johnson said it
  was the triumph of hope over experience. —Samuel Johnson

MARCH 28

- *Don't fire until you see the whites of their eyes.* —Israel Putnam
- *The greatest prayer is patience.* —Lord Buddha
- *Prejudice is the reason of fools.* —Voltaire
- *A friend is a person with whom I may be sincere.*
  Before him, I may think aloud. —IBID
- *It's better to have fought and lost, than never to have fought at all.*
  —Arthur Hugh Clough
- *Come live with me and be my love,*
  and we will all the pleasures prove
  that valleys, groves, hills, and fields,
  woods or steep mountain yields. —Christopher Marlowe
- *A good laugh is sunshine in a house.* —Thackeray
- *Teach your child to hold his tongue,*
  he'll learn fast enough to speak. —Franklin

MARCH 29

- *I pledge you, I pledge myself to a new deal for the American people.*

  —Franklin D. Roosevelt

- *The man who dies rich dies disgraced.* —Andrew Carnegie
- *Rich men have no faults.* —Proverb
- *May God defend me from my friends;*
  I can defend myself from my enemies. —Duc De Villars
- *In spite of all the yearnings of men, no one can produce a single fact or reason to support the belief in God and in personal immortality.*

  —Clarence Darrow

- *As I was going up the stair,*
  I met a man who wasn't there.
  He wasn't there again today.
  I wish, I wish he'd stay away. —Hughes Mearns

MARCH 30

- *We are as the king, only not as rich.* —Anonymous
- *The ways to enrich are many, most of them foul.* —Francis Bacon
- *The only thing we have to fear is fear itself.* —Franklin D. Roosevelt
- *If poetry comes not as naturally as leaves to a tree,*
  it had better not come at all. -John Keats
- *Now, Dasher! now, Dancer! now, Prancer and Vixen! On,*
  comet! on, Cupid! on Dunder and Blitzen! —IBID
- *From childhood's hour I have not been*
  as others were I have not seen
  as others saw. —Eogar Allan Poe

MARCH 31

- *I will not accept if nominated and will not serve if elected.*

—William Sherman

- *A revolution is legality on vacation.* —Leon Blum
- *That man is the richest whose pleasures are the cheapest.* —Thoreau
- *Ten measures of beauty came into the world;*
  Jerusalem received nine measures and the rest of the world one.

—Anonymous

- *It is an accustomed action with her to seem thus*
  washing her hands. I have known her continue in
  this a quarter of an hour. —IBID
- *This is better, that one do*
  his own task as he may, even though he fail,
  than take task not his own, though they seem good
  to die performing duty is no ill;
  but who seeks others, roads shall wander still. —Gita
- *Adam ate the apple, and our teeth still ache.* —Hungarian Proverb
- *Six years of experiment have showed me that*
  the of ideal food is fresh fruit and nuts.

—Mohan Das Karamchand Gandhi

APRIL

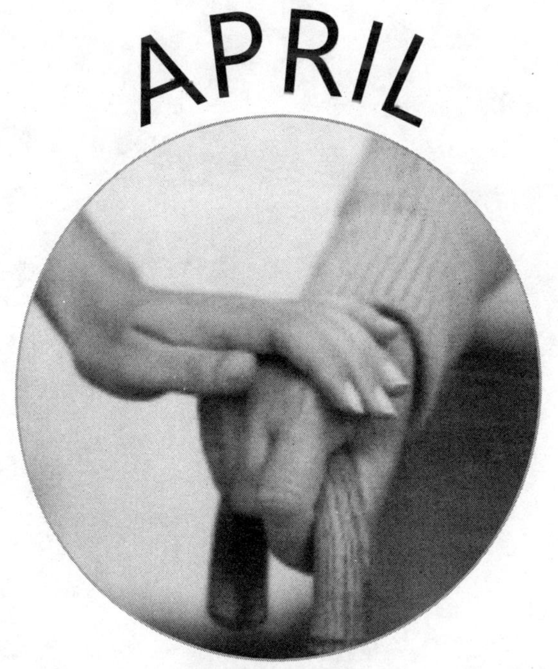

Spirit

to serve

APRIL 1

- *Go west young man, go west.* —John B.L. Soule
- *Revolutions are not about trifles, but spring from trifles.* —Aristotle
- *The rich knows not who his friend is.* —Proverb
- *A wife loves out of duty, and duty leads to constraint, and constraint kills desire.* —Jean Giraudoux
- *Art thou but a dagger of the mind, a false creation proceeding from the heat-oppressed brain?* —IBID

APRIL 2

- *Revolutions are not made; they come.* —Wendell Philips
- *Every revolution was first a thought in one man's mind.* —R.W. Emerson
- *I'm going to fight hard. I'm going to give them hell.* —Harry S. Truman
- *One was never married, and that's his hell; another is, and that's his plague.* —Robert Burton
- *I never forget a face, but in your case I'll make an exception.* —Groucho Marx
- *True genius resides in the capacity for evaluation of uncertain, hazardous, and conflicting information.* —Winston Churchill
- *I think it can be stated without denial that no man ever saw a man he would be willing to marry if he were a woman.* —George Gibbs

APRIL 3

- *The eyes of all people are upon us.* —John Winthrop
- *Fame is a magnifying glass.* —Proverb
- *Hold a true friend with both your hands.* —Nigerian Proverb
- *Against a foe I can myself defend*
  but heaven protect me from a blundering friend.
  —D.W. Thompson
- *Character is always known. Thefts never enrich; alms never improverish; murder will speak out of stone walls.* —Ralph Waldo Emerson
- *It is a truth universally acknowledged,*
  that a single man in possession of good fortune,
  must be in want of a wife. —Jane Austen

APRIL 4

- *America is God's crucible, the great melting pot.* —Israel Zangwill
- *The future is made of the same stuff as the present.* —Simone Weil
- *Advice is seldom welcome, those who need it most like it least.*
  —Samuel Johnson
- *True friendship is like sound health;*
  the value of it is seldom known until it be lost. —C.C. Colton
- *Cherchez la femme. Find the woman.* —Joseph Fouche
- *When a woman gets married,*
  it's like jumping into a hole in the ice in the middle of winter.
  You do it once and you remember it the rest of your days. —Maxim Gorky

APRIL 5

- *What a glorious morning for America!* —Samuel Adams
- *I know of no way of judging the future but by the past.* —Patrick Henry
- *Never give advice in a crowd.* —Arab Proverb
- *Friendship is the shadow of the evening,*
  which strengthens with the setting sun of life. —Fuller
- *Polygamy may well be held in dread, not only as a sin but as a bore.*
  —Lord Byron
- *Civilisation begins with order,*
  grows with liberty
  and dies with chaos.
  —Will Durant

APRIL 6

- *Declare the United States the winner and begin de-escalation.*
  —Sen. George Aiken
- *Fear of ideas makes us impotent and ineffective.* —William O. Douglas
- *I never think of the future. It comes soon enough.* —Albert Einstein
- *Trust no future, howe'er pleasant!*
  Let the dead past bury its dead! —Lohgfellow
- *How often when men are at the point of death*
  Have they been merry! —Shakespeare
- *Marriage is a result of the longing for the deep,*
  deep peace of the double bed after the hurly-burly of the chaise longue.
  —Patrick Campbell
- *Marriage is for woman the commonest mode of livelihood*
  and the total amount of undesired sex endured by women
  is probably greater in marriage than in prostitution. —Bertrand Russell

APRIL 7

- *Let us not be deceived-we are today in the midst of a cold war.*
  —Bernard Baruch
- *The only thing we have to fear is fear itself.* —Franklin D. Roosevelt
- *Ignorance of future ills is a more useful thing than knowledge.* —Cicero
- *The actions of men are like the index to a book;*
  they point out what is most remarkable in them.—Thomas Fuller
- *Marriage is popular because it combines the*
  maximum of temptation with the maximum of opportunity.
  —IBID
- *Some men are born mediocre, some men achieve mediocrity,*
  and some men have mediocrity thrust upon them.
  With major it had been all three. —Joseph Heller

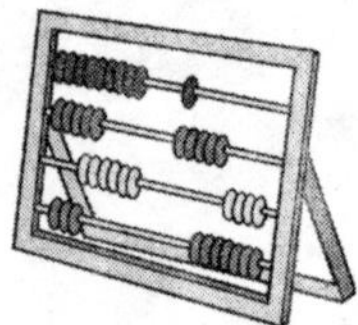

APRIL 8

- *Bury my heart at wounded knee.* —Stephen Vincent Benet
- *The first duty of man is that of subduing fear.* —Thomas Carlyle
- *Tomorrow is always the busiest day of the week.* —Jonathan Lazear
- *When all else is lost, the future still remains.* —Bovee
- *Right action cannot come out of nothing,*
  it must be preceded by thought. —Jawaharlal Nehru
- *The world has grown suspicious of anything*
  that looks like a happy married life. —Oscar Wilde
- *I have a rendezvous with death the ancient saying is no heresy,*
  not louder shrieks to pitying heaven are cast,
  when husbands or when lapdogs breathe their last.
  —Alexander Pope

APRIL 9

- *The chief business of the American people is business.* —Calvin Cooudge
- *Let us fear God and we shall cease to fear man.* —M. K. Gandhi
- *Love is blind; friendship closes its eyes.* —Proverb
- *Get good counsel before you begin; and when you have decided, act promptly.* —Sallust
- *Death is the veil which those who live call life: they sleep and it is lifted.* —Percy Bysshe Shelley
- *The long dull monotonous years of middle-aged prosperity or middle-aged adversity are excellent campaigning weather for the devil.* —C.S. Lewis

APRIL 10

- *All or nothing.* —Henrik Ibsen
- *Every noble activity makes room for itself.* —Emerson
- *Be concerned with actions only, never with its results.* —Yajur Veda
- *Heav'n from all creatures hides the Book of Fate, all but the page prescribed, their present state.* —Pope
- *Whoever, in middle age, attempts to realize the wishes and hopes of his early youth invariably deceives himself. Each ten years of a man's life has it own fortunes, its own hopes, its own desires.* —Goethe

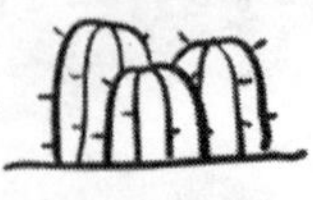

APRIL 11

- *America is a country of young men.* —Ralph Waldo Emerson
- *Fear has many eyes and can see things underground.* —Miguel De Cervantes
- *The principal mark of genius is not perfection but originality,*
  the opening of new frontiers. —Arthur Koestler
- *Men must endure*
  their going hence even as their coming hither. —Shakespeare
- *By the time a person has achieved years adequate for choosing a direction, the die is cast and the moment has long since passed which determined the future.* —Zelda Fitzgerald

APRIL 12

- *There are no second acts in American lives.* —F. Scott Fitzgerald
- *No rule is so general, which admits not some exception.* —Robert Burton
- *Action speaks louder than words.* —English Proverb
- *Little deeds of kindness, little words of love,*
  help to make earth happy, like to heaven above. —Julia Carney
- *We give advice by the bucket, but take it by the grain.* —W.R. Alger
- *Sigh no more, ladies, sigh no more,*
  men were deceivers ever;
  One foot in sea, and one on shore,
  to one thing constant never. —Shakespeare
- *The sunlight claps the earth*
  and the moonbeams kiss the sea.
  What are all these kissing worth?
  If you kiss not me? —P.B. Shelley
- *What governs men is the fear of truth.* —Henri Frederic Amie

APRIL 13

- *The American system of rugged individualism.* —Herbert Hoover
- *The great end of life is not knowledge but action.* —Thomas Henry Huxley
- *To accept good advice is but to increase one's ability.* —Goethe
- *Old people love to give good advice;*
  it compensates them for their inability to set a bad example. —La Rochefoucauld
- *For a people who are free, and who mean to remain so,*
  a well-organized and armed militia is their best security. —Thomas Jefferson
- *And a day less or more at sea or shore, we die-does it matter when?* —Alfred Lord Tennyson

APRIL 14

- *Hitch your wagon to a star.* —Ralph Waldo Emerson
- *Strong reasons make strong actions.* —Shakespeare
- *Actions are ours; their consequences belong to heaven.* —Sir P. Francis
- *Tis the sunset of life gives me mystical lore,*
  and coming events cast their shadows before. —Campbell
- *Democracy is the worst form of government except all those*
  other forms that have been tried from tune to tune. —Winston Churchill
- *The good die first,*
  and they whose hearts are dry as summer dust
  burn to the socket. —William Wordsworth
- *Nothing in life is to be feared.*
  It is only to be understood. —Marie Curie

APRIL 15

- *Death is not an event in life; we do not experience death.*
  —Ludwig Wittgenstein
- *Never give advice unless asked.* —German Proverb
- *Many receive advice, only the wise profit by it.* —Publilius Syrus
- *I have found the best way to give advice to your children is to find out what they want and them advise them to do it.*
  —Harry S. Truman
- *First say to yourself what you would be; and then do what you have to do.* —Epictetus
- *Every citizen should be a soldier. This was the case with the Greeks and the Romans, and must be that of every free state.*
  —Thomas Jefferson

APRIL 16

- *I would sooner fail than not be among the greatest.* —John Keats
- *Charity begins at home, is the voice of the world.* —Thomas Browne
- *Fear follows crime and is its punishment.* —Francois Marie Voltaire
- *All that live must die, passing through nature to eternity.* —Shakespeare
- *Animals are such agreeable friends - they ask no questions, they pass no criticisms.* —George Eliot
- *Man comes and tills the field and lies beneath, and after many a summer dies the swan.* —Alfred
- *Do not go gentle into that good night, old age should burn and rave at close of day; Rage, rage against the dying of the light.* —Dylan Thomas

APRIL 17

- *Indeed I tremble for my country when I reflect that God is just.*

  —Thomas Jefferson
- *To keep a lamp burning we have to keep putting oil in it.*

  —Mother Teresa
- *The living need charity more than the dead.* —George Amold
- *The greatest genius is never so great as when it is chastised and subdued by the highest reason.* —Charles Caleb Colton
- *I neglect God and his Angels for the noise of a fly, for the rattling of a coach, for the whining of a door.*

  —John Donne
- *Discipline is the soul of an army.*
  It makes small numbers formidable;
  procures success to the weak and esteem to all. —George Washington

APRIL 18

- *I am willing to love all mankind, except an American.* —Samuel Johnson
- *All that is worth remembering of life is the poetry of it.* —William Hazlitt
- *Poetry is the art of uniting pleasure with truth.* —Samuel Johnson
- *Politics is the art of preventing people from taking part in affairs which properly concern them.* —Paul Valery
- *My days are swifter than a weaver's shuttle,*
  and are spent without hope. —Bible
- *Half a league, half a league,*
  half a league onward,
  All in the valley of death
  rode the six hundred. —Alfred

APRIL 19

- *It is more blessed to give than to receive.* —Bible
- *Poetry is the rhythmical creation of beauty in words.* —Edgar Allan Poe
- *If I like it, I say its mine. If I don't, I say it's a fake.* —Pablo Picasso
- *The moment the idea is admitted into society that property is not as sacred as the laws of God ...... anarchy and tyranny commence.*

  —John Adams
- *What we call a mind is nothing but a heap or*
  collection of different perceptions, united together
  by certain relations, and supposed, though falsely,
  to be endowed with a perfect simplicity and identity.

  —David Hume

APRIL 20

- *Nothing is permanent except change.* —Heraclitus
- *God loveth a cheerful giver.* —Bible
- *He best can paint them who shall feel them most.* —Alexander Pope
- *When one is painting, one does not think.* —Raphael
- *The interest of those who own the property used in industry ...... is that their capital should be dear and human beings cheap.*

  —R.H. Tawney
- *I do not want people to be very agreeable,*
  as it saves me the trouble of liking them a great deal.

  —Jane Austen
- *I do not love thee, Doctor Fell.*
  The reason why I cannot tell.
  But this alone I know full well.
  I do not love thee, Doctor Fell. —Thomas Brown

APRIL 21

- *He is rich who hath enough to be charitable.* —Sir Thomas Browne
- *I paint objects as I think, them, not as I see them.* —Pablo Picasso
- *Every time I paint a portrait I lose a friend.* —John Singe
- *In most countries, people grow fiercely possessive of their property. It is a bastion of conservatism.* —Gordon W. Allport
- *Nothing in his life Became him like the leaving it.* —Shakespeare
- *I knew once a very covetous, sordid fellow, who used to say, "Take care of the pence, for the pounds will take care of themselves".* —Earl of Chesterfield

APRIL 22

- *When the going gets tough, the tough get going.* —Joe Kennedy
- *Have no friends not equal to yourself.* —Confucius
- *There are no illegitimate children-only illegitimate parents.* —Leonr
- *Yet who would have thought the old man to have hud so much blood in him?* —Shakespeare
- *Old fools are more foolish than young ones.* —La Rache Foucauld
- *Money, it turned out, was exactly like sex. You thought of nothing else if you did'nt have it and thought of other things if you did.* —James Baldwin

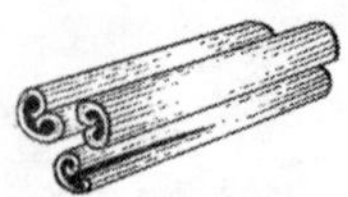

APRIL 23

- *Cast thy bread upon the waters.* —Bible
- *Nothing succeeds like success.* —Proverb
- *Confession is good for the soul.* —Scottish Proverb
- *A true friend is the most precious of an possession and the one we take the least thought about acquiring.*
  —La Rochefoucauld
- *Murder most foul, as in the best it is,*
  but this most foul, strange and unnatural. —Shakespeare
- *In the nightmare of the dark*
  all the dogs of Europe bark
  and the living nations wait,
  each sequestered in its hate. —W. H. Auden

APRIL 24

- *The wind of change is blowing through this continent.*
  —Harold Macmillan
- *The eyes are the windows of the soul.* —Proverb
- *Real beauty is the beauty of soul.* —M.K. Gandhi
- *If a man does not make new acquaintances as he advances through life, he will soon find himself-left alone.*
  —Samuel Johnson
- *Democracy substitutes election by the incompetent many for appointment by the corrupt few.* —George Bernard Shaw
- *The human species, according to the best theory*
  I can form of it, is composed of two distinct races,
  the men who borrow and the men who lend. —Charles Lamb

APRIL 25

- *The basic fact of today is the tremendous pace of change in human life.* —Jawaharlal Nehru
- *The soul is not where it lives, but where it loves.* —Proverb
- *Silence is one great art of conversation.* —Hazlitt
- *The most stringent protection of free speech would not protect a man from falsely shouting fire in a theater and causing a panic.* —Gliver
- *I was much further out than you thought and-not waving but drowning.* —Stevie Smith
- *Tomorrow, and tomorrow; and tomorrow, creeps in this petty pace from day to day, to the last! syllable of recorded time.* —Shakespeare

APRIL 26

- *You can't step twice into the same river.* —Heraclitus
- *Speech is the index of the mind.* —Seneca
- *When you win, nothing hurts.* —Joe Namath
- *An enunciated today, 'Progress' is simply a comparative of which we have not settled the superlative* —G. K. Chesterton
- *It has long been an axiom of mine that the little things are infinitely the most important* —A Conan Doyle
- *A little neglect may breed great mischief... for the want of a nail the shoe was lost, for the want of a shoe the horse was lost; and for the want of a horse the rider was lost.* —Benjamin Franklin

APRIL 27

- *Everything flows, nothing stays still;* —Heraclitus
- *Time and tide wait for no man.* —English Proverb
- *Time past cannot be recalled.* —Proverb
- *Hide not your thoughts. If it is shameful to reveal them, it is more shameful to think them.* —M. K. Gandhi
- *Large streams from little fountains flow, tall oaks from little acorns grow.* —David Everett
- *Money is a singular thing. It ranks with love as man's greatest source of joy. And with his death as his greatest source of anxiety.*

  —John Kenneth Galbraith

APRIL 28

- *Nothing is permanent but change.* —Heraclitus
- *Silence is sometimes the severest criticism.* —Charles Buxton
- *Victory has a hundred fathers but defeat is an orphan.* —C.G. Ciano
- *Thinking is the hardest work there is, which is the probable reason why so few engage in it.*

  —Henry Ford
- *Wisdom consists in being able to distinguish among dangers and make a choice of the least harmful.*

  —Machiavelli
- *Annual income twenty pounds, annual expenditure nineteen pounds six, result happiness. Annual income twenty pounds, annual expenditure twenty pounds ought and six, result misery.*

  —Charles Dickens

APRIL 29

- *Assassination is the extreme form of censorship.*—George Bernard Shaw
- *God made time, but man made haste.* —Irish Proverb
- *The only soul a man must save is his own.* —William Douglas
- *Every tear from every eye*
  babe in eternity. —Blake
- *Yond Cassius has a lean and hungry look; he thinks too much : such men are dangerous.* —IBID
- *In order to stand well in the eyes of the community, it is necessary to come up to a certain, somewhat indefinite, conventional standard of wealth.* —Thorstein Veblen

APRIL 30

- *Much effort, much prosperity.* —Euripides
- *If folly were grief, every house would weep.* —Proverb
- *Speech without the backing of experience based on action will lack chastity and refinement.* —M. K. Gandhi
- *The bird of time has but a little way*
  to flutter-and the bird is on the wing. —Omar
- *There is a feeling of eternity in youth which makes amends for everything. To be young is to be as one of the immortals.* —William Hazlitt
- *Hatred is like fire; it makes even light rubbish deadly.* —George Eliot

Ability

to achieve

MAY 1

- *We write frankly and freely but we "modify" before we print.* —Mark Twain
- *Time is money.* —Bulwer-lytton
- *If you would have me weep, you must feel grief yourself.* —Horace
- *Thinking is easy, acting is difficult, and to put one's thoughts into action is the most difflcult thing in the world.* —Goethe
- *The difficult we do immediately. The impossible takes a little longer.* —U.S. Army Corps of Engineers
- *If I should die, think only this of me; That there's some corner of a foreign field that is forever England.* —Rupeh Brooke

MAY 2

- *Nature's mighty law is change.* —Robert Burns
- *Success has made failure of many men.* —Cindy Adams
- *Time is a great healer.* —Proverb
- *Silence is often the best answer.* —Anonymous
- *For my thoughts are not your thoughts, neither are your ways, my ways.* —Old Testament
- *Soap and education are not as sudden so a massacre, but they are more deadly in the long run.* —Mark Twain
- *The boundaries of democracy have to be widened so as to include economic equality also. This is the great revolution through which we are all passing.* —Jawaharlal Nehru

MAY 3

- *Change is inevitable in a progressive society. Change is constant.*
  —Benjamin Disraeli
- *Fatigue is the best pillow.* —Franklin
- *Silence is more eloquent than words.* —T. Carlyle
- *Man is but a reed, the weakest in nature, but he is a thinking reed.*
  —Pascal
- *Training is everything. The peach was once a bitter almond; cauliflower is nothing but a cabbage with a college education.*
  —Mark Twain
- *Everything ponderous, viscous and solemnly clumsy, all long-winded and boring types of style are developed in profuse variety among Germans.* —Friedrich Nietzsche

MAY 4

- *The revolution eats its own. Capitalism recreates itself.*
  —Mordecai Rjchler
- *There is a time and place for everything.* —Proverb
- *Never a tear bedims the eye that time and patience will not dry.* —Bret Harte
- *Education.... has produced a vast population able to read but unable to distinguish what is worth reading.*
  —G.M. Trevelyan
- *Mysticism is, in essence, little more than a certain intensity and depth of feeling in regard to what is believed about the universe.* —Bertrand Russell
- *The wind of change is blowing through this Continent, and whether we like it or not, this growth of national consciousness is a political fact.* —Harold Macmillan

MAY 5

- *The public be damned! I'm working for my stockholders.*
  —William Henry V Anderbilt
- *A little body doth often harbour a great soul.* —English Proverb
- *Life is perennial search for truth.* —Yajur Veda
- *I would I could stand on a busy comer, a hat in hand,*
  and beg people to throw me all their wasted hours.
  —Bernard Berenson
- *There is no king who has not had a slave among his ancestors,*
  and no slave who has not had a king among his. —Helen Keller
- *Whatever nature has in store for mankind,*
  unpleasant as it may be, men must accept,
  for ignorance is never better than knowledge. —Enrico Fermi

MAY 6

- *Property is organised robbery.* —George Bernard Shaw
- *To choose time is to save time.* —Francis Bacon
- *A harmful truth is better than a useful lie.* —Thomas Mann
- *One must be poor to know the luxury of giving.* —George Eliot
- *Our faults irritate us most when we see them in others.* —Duch Proverb
- *Nothing really belongs to us but time,*
  which even he has who has nothing else. —Bal Thasar Gracian
- *To consider onself different from ordinary men is wrong,*
  but it is right to hope that one will not remain like ordinary men.
  —Yoshida shoin
- *To see a world in a grain of sand*
  and a heaven in wild flower,
  hold infinity in the palm of your hand
  and eternity in an hour. —William Blake

MAY 7

- *The first requisite to happiness is to be born in a famous city.* —Euripides
- *Success is a journey, not a destination.* —Ben Sweetland
- *Time tries all things.* —Proverb
- *I recommend you to take care of the minutes, for the hours will take care of themselves.* —Chestelfield
- *Men are all alike in their promises. It is only in their deeds that they differ.* —Moliere
- *This agglomeration which was called and still calls itself the Holt Roman Empire was neither holy, nor roman, nor an empire in any way.* —Voltaire

MAY 8

- *What is the city but the people?* —Shakespeare
- *Victory has a hundred memories but defeat has amnesia.* —W.I.E. Gates
- *Truth is mighty and will prevail.* —Thomas Brooks
- *Time goes, you say? Ah no! Alas, Time stays, we go.* —Austin Dobson
- *Patience is the art of hoping.* —Vauvenargues
- *People who do not believe in miracles are not realistic.* —David Ben-Gurion
- *We become just by performing just actions, temperate by performing temperate actions, brave by performing brave actions.* —Aristotle
- *That's the wise thrush; he sings each song twice over, lest you think he never could recapture the first fine careless rapture!* —Robert Browning

MAY 9

- *On the whole I'd rather be in Philadelphia.* —W. C. Fields
- *The unspoken word never does harm.* —Kossuth
- *Truth is simple and easy. Falsehood is devious :*
it could well be the cause of destruction. —Rig Veda
- *Cured yesterday of my disease,*
I died last night of the physician. —Matthew Prior
- *The earth and ocean seem*
to sleep it! one another's arms, and dream
of waves, flowers, clouds, woods, rocks, and all
that we read in their smiles, and call reality.
—Percy Bysshe Shelley

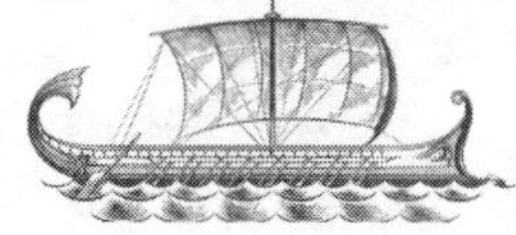

MAY 10

- *Water is best.* —Pindar
- *Even a fool, when he holdeth his peace, is counted wise.*
—Old Testament
- *Silence, along with modesty, is a great aid to conversation.*
—Montaigne
- *One cannot reach truth, by untruthfulness.*
Truthful conduct alone can reach truth. —M.K. Gandhi
- *The greatest happiness of the greatest number is the*
foundation of morals and legislation. —Jeremy Bentham
- *I demonstrate by means of philosophy that the*
earth is round and is inhabited on all sides;
that it is insignificantly small, and is borne through the stars.
—Johann Kepler

MAY 11

- *It's a long time between drinks.* —Robert Louis Stevenson
- *Silence is the safety zone of conversation.* —Arnold Glasow
- *Silence is wisdom and gets friends.* —Proverb
- *A half-truth won far ourselves is worth more than a whole truth learned from others.* —S. Radhakrishnan
- *No morality can be founded on authority, even if the authority were divine.* —A. J. Ayer
- *All nature is but art, unknown to thee;*
  all chance, direction, which thou canst not see;
  all discord, harmony not understood;
  all partial evil, universal good. —Alexander Pope

MAY 12

- *To be vanquished and yet not surrender, that is victory.* —Josef Pilsudski
- *Silence shows consent.* —Proverb
- *Winning is overemphasized. The only time it is really important is in surgery and war.* —Ai Mcguire
- *Drink no longer water, but use a little wine for thy stomach's sake and thine often infirmities.* —Bible
- *Dogs display reluctance and wrath*
  if you try to give them a bath
  they bury bones in hideaways
  and half the time they trot sideaways. —Ogden Nash

MAY 13

- *There are so few who can grow old with a good grace.* —Richard Steele
- *Such another victory and we are ruined.* —Pyrrhus
- *The smile of God is victory.* —Whittier
- *I always say that, next to a battle lost, the greatest misery is a battle gained.* —Duke of Wellington
- *Time swallows up everything that is visible, sparing nothing. It does not spare even outstanding personalities.* —Shri Rama
- *If he does really think that there is no distinction between virture and vice, why, Sir, when he leaves our houses, let us count our spoons.* —Samuel Johnson

MAY 14

- *Every man desires to live long, but no man would be old.* —Jonathan Swift
- *Silence seldom doth ham.* —English Proverb
- *Science is the refusal to believe on the basis of hope.* —C. P. Snow
- *Power comes from sincere service.* —M. K. Gandhi
- *Truth is a jewel which should not be painted over; but it may be set to advantage and shown in a good light.* —George Santayana
- *I know only that what is moral is what you feel good after and what is immoral is what you feel bad after.* —Ernest Hemingway
- *The greatest pleasure of a dog is that you may make a fool of yourself with him and not only will he not scold you, but he will make a fool of himself too.* —Samuel Butler

MAY 15

- *Old age is the most unexpected of all the things that can happen to a man.* —Leon Trotsky
- *The magic of property turns sand to gold.* —Jeremy Benthan
- *To make headway, improve your head.* —B. C. Forbes
- *The biggest problem in the world, could have been solved when it was small.* —Witter Bynner
- *No actions are bad in themselves— even murder can be justified.* —Dietrich Bonhoeffer
- *So, naturalists observe, a flea*
  hath smaller fleas that on him prey;
  And these have smaller fleas to bite em
  and so proceed ad infinitum. —Jonathan Swift

MAY 16

- *The tragedy of old age is not that one is old. But that one is young.* —Oscar Wilde
- *Property is theft.* —P.J. Proudhon
- *The wicked flee when no man pursuit.* —Bible
- *There is a time of speaking and a time of being still.* —William Caxton
- *Some for renown, on scraps of learning dote,*
  and think they grow immortal as they quote. —Edward Young
- *The number of people in possession of any criteria for discriminating between good and evil is very small.* —T.S. Eliot
- *If a dog jumps in your lap, it is because he is fond of you; but if a cat does the same thing, it is because your lap is warmer.* —Alfred North Whitehead

MAY 17

- *For you and I are past our dancing days.* —Shakespeare
- *Is it progress if a cannibal uses knife and fork?* —S. J. Lec
- *Property has its duties as well as its rights.* —T. Drummond
- *Those who speak most of progress measure it by quantity and not by quality.* —George Santayana
- *"Do the duty which lies nearest thee", which thou knowest to be a duty! Thy second duty will already have become clearer.* —Thomas Carlyle
- *Woodman, spare-that tree!*
  Touch not a single bough!
  In youth it sheltered me,
  and I'll protect it now. —George Pope Morris

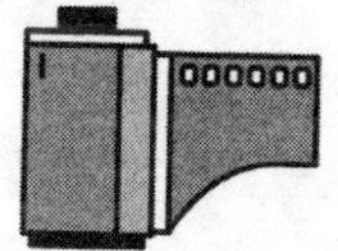

MAY 18

- *Nobody loves life like him who is growing old.* —Sophocles
- *The latter end of joy is woe.* —Geoffrey Chaucer
- *All seek joy, but it is not found on earth.* —ST. John Chrysostom
- *Crime, like virtue, has its degrees.* —Racine
- *It is neither wealth nor splendor, but tranquillity and occupation, which give happiness.* —Thomas Jefferson
- *It doesn't matter what you do, as long as you don't do it in public and frighten the horses.* —Mrs. Patrick Campbell
- *I think I could turn and live with animals,*
  they are so placid and self-contained,
  I stand and look at them long and long. —Walt Whitman

MAY 19

- *Being seventy is not a sin.* —Golda Meir
- *To live happily is an inward power of the soul.* —Marcus Aurelius
- *Ask yourself whether you are happy, and you will cease to be so.*
  —John Stuart Mill
- *The secret of happiness is to face the fact that*
  the world is horrible, horrible, horrible. —Bertrand Russell
- *Oh that I had wings like a dove! for then*
  I would flyaway, and be at rest. —Bible
- *Consider the lilies of the field, how they grow;*
  they toil not neither do they spin;
  And yet I say unto you, that even solomon in all
  his glory was not arrayed like one of these. —Bible

MAY 20

- *One aged man-one man-can't fill a house.* —Robert Frost
- *Our happiness depends on wisdom all the way.* —Sophocles
- *One is never as fortunate or as unfortunate as one imagines.*
  —La Rochefoucauld
- *The world is so full of a number of things,*
  I'm sure we should all be as happy as kings. —R.L. Stevenson
- *Listen; there's a hell of a good universe next door. Let's go.*
  —E.E. Cummings
- *There is something about the unselfish and self-sacrificing*
  love of a brute, which goes directly to the heart of him
  who has had frequent occasion to test the paltry friendship
  and gossamer fidelity of mere man. —Edgar Allan Poe

MAY 21

- *When we ask advice, we are usually looking for an accomplice.*

  —Marquis De Lagrange
- *Nothing is more powerful than habit.* *—Ovid*
- *Where guilt is, rage and courage doth abound.* *—Ben Jonson*
- *Habit is a second nature that prevents us from knowing the first, of which it has neither the cruelties nor the enchantments.*

  —Proust
- *The world has achieved brilliance without conscience. Ours is a world of nuclear giants and ethical infants.*

  —Omar Bradley
- *The kiss of the sun for pardon,*
  the song of the birds for mirth.
  One is nearer God's heart in a garden
  than anywhere else on earth.

  —Dorothy Gurney

MAY 22

- *One gives nothing so freely as advice.* *—La Rochefoucauld*
- *The great man is he who does not lose his child's heart.* *—Mencius*
- *Great men can't be ruled.* *—Ayn Rand*
- *The difference between my quotations and those of the next man is that I leave out the inverted commas.* *—George Moore*
- *No one can be perfectly free till all are free;*
  no one can be perfectly moral till all are moral;
  on one can be perfectly happy till all are happy. *—Herbert Spencer*

MAY 23

- *People ask you for criticism, but they only want praise.* —W. Somersetmaugam
- *The guilty think all talk is of themselves.* —Chaucer
- *Women and Horses and Power and War.* —Rudyard Kipling
- *The wisdom of the wise and the experience of the ages are perpetuated by quotation.* —Benjamin Disraeli
- *Whoever fights monsters should see to it that in the process he does not become a monster. And when you look long into an abyss, the abyss also looks into you.* —Friedrich Nietzsche

MAY 24

- *Old men are always young enough to learn, with profit.* —Aeschylus
- *The art of reading is to skip judiciously.* —P. G. Hamerton
- *The religion of one seems madness unto another.* —Thomas Browne
- *I think we must ... quote whenever we feel that the allusion is interesting or helpful of amusing.* —Clifton Fadiman
- *Ethical metaphysics is fundamentally an attempt, however disguised, to give legislative force to our own wishes.* —Bertrand Russell
- *Roll on, thou deep and dark blue ocean roll*
  ten thousand fleets sweep over thee in vain;
  Man marks the earth with ruin-his control
  stops with the shore. —Lord Byron

MAY 25

- *To me, old age is always fifteen years older than I am.*
  —Bernard Baruch
- *Emotion has taught mind to reason.* —Marquisde Vauvenargues
- *Good reason must, of force, give place to better.* —Shakespeare
- *If you make people think they're thinking, they'll love you;*
  but if you really make them think, they 'll hate you.
  —Don Marquis
- *Evil is unspectacular and always human*
  and shares our bed and eats at our own table. —W. H. Auden
- *So farewell hope, and with hope farewell fear,*
  farewell remorse; all good to me is lost; Evil be thou my good.
  —John Milton

MAY 26

- *Good but rarely came from good advice.* —Lord Byron
- *The heart has reasons of which reason has no knowledge.* —Pascal
- *Reason rules all things.* —Proverb
- *Never reason from what you do not know. If you do,*
  you will soon believe what is utterly against reason —Ramsay
- *Morality is not properly that doctrine of how we may make*
  ourselves happy, but how we may make ourselves
  worthy of happiness. —Immanuel Kant
- *A primrose by a river's brim,*
  a yellow primrose was to him,
  And it was nothing more. —William Wordsworth

MAY 27

- *How old would you be if you didn't know how old you was?* —Satchel Paige
- *And God said unto Moses, I AM THAT I AM.* —Bible
- *To fall into a habit is to begin to cease to be.* —Miguel De unamuno
- *A is flies-to wanton boys are we to the gods*
  they kill us for their sport. —Shakespeare
- *The older I grow, the more I distrust the*
  familiar doctrine that age brings wisdom. —H. L. Mencken
- *I wandered lonely as a cloud*
  that floats on high o'er vales and hills,
  When all at once I saw a crowd,
  a host of golden daffodils. —William Wordsworth

MAY 28

- *Dancing is just discovery, discovery, discovery.* —Martha Graham
- *Sleep is the best cure for waking troubles.* —Cervantes
- *Truth is always the strongest argument.* —Sophocles
- *Awake my soul, and with the sun*
  the daily stage of duty run. —Thomas Ken
- *Wickedness is always ever than virtue;*
  for it takes the short cut to everything. —Samuel Johnson
- *'Tis the last rose of summer left blooming alone;*
  All her lovely companions are faded and gone. —Thomas Moore

MAY 29

- *Dance is the hidden language of the soul.* —IBID
- *A god does not change his ways.* —Tertullian
- *The Lord is my shepherd; I shall not want.* —Bible
- *There's a mighty big difference between good,*
  sound reasons and reasons that sound good. —Burton Hillis
- *The facts are to blame my friend. We are all imprisoned by facts.* —Luigi Pirandello
- *It snowed and snowed, the whole world over,*
  snow swept the world from end to end.
  A candle burned on the table;
  A candle burned. —Boris Pasternak

MAY 30

- *If the king loves music, there is little wrong in the land.* —Mencius
- *The sleep of a labouring man is sweet.* —Ecclesiastes
- *The vigorous are no better than the lazy during one half of life,*
  for all men are alike when asleep. —Aristotle
- *If one good deed in all my life I did,*
  I do repent it from my very soul. —Shakespeare
- *April is the cruellest month, breeding*
  lilacs out of the dead land, mixing
  memory and desire, stirring
  dull roots with spring rain. —T.S. Eliot

MAY 31

- *All art constantly aspires towards the conditions of music.*
  —Walter Pater
- *Judge none blessed before his death.* —Bible
- *The joyfulness of a man prolongeth his days.* —IBID
- *This is the technique of the soul.*
  The individual must die so that the nation must live.
  —Subhash Chandra Bose
- *There is a capacity of virtue in us,*
  and there is a capacity of vice to make your blood creep.
  —Ralph Waldo Emerson
- *Science is nothing but perception.* —Plato
- *Men loved darkness rather than light,*
  because their deeds were evil. —Bible
- *Responsibility is the high price of self ownership.* —Hans Clarin
- *Silence is the safety zone of conversation.* —Arnold Glasow
- *Stability is not immobility.* —Metternich
- *Success usually comes to those who are too busy to be looking for it.*
  —Henry David Thoreau
- *You only live once, but if you do it right, once is enough.* —Mae West
- *Get busy living or get busy dying.* —Stephen King
- *Twenty years from now you will be more disappointed by the things that you did not do than by the ones you did do.*
  —Mark Twain

JUNE

Aim

to succeed

JUNE 1

- *If music be the food of love, play on.* —Shakespeare
- *One hour's sleep before midnight is worth two after.* —Proverb
- *War is the business of barbarians.* —Napoleon
- *Oh sleep! it is a gentle thing,*
  beloved from pole to pole. —Samuel Taylor Coleridge
- *The evil that men do lives after them,*
  the good is oft interred with their bones. —Shakespeare
- *In winter I get up by night and dress by yellow candlelight.*
  In summer quite the other way,
  I have to go to bed by day. —Robert Louis Stevenson

JUNE 2

- *I am never merry when I hear sweet music.* —Shakespeare
- *A good wife makes a good husband.* —Proverb
- *Wisdom is to the soul what health is to the body.* —Anonymous
- *Recommend to your children virtue;*
  that alone can make them happy, not gold. —Beethoven
- *War is a dangerous teacher and physical victory*
  leads often to a moral defeat. —Shri Aurobindo
- *If a man write a better book, preach a better sermon,*
  or make a better mousetrap than his neighbour, tho' he
  build his house in the woods, the world will make a
  beaten path to his door. —Ralph Waldo Emerson

JUNE 3

- *Hell is full of musical amateurs.* —George Bernard Shaw
- *Virtue is its own reward.* —Cicero
- *In youth and beauty wisdom is but rare!* —Homer
- *Virtue is an angel, but she is a blind one and must ask of knowledge to show her the pathway that leads to her goal.* —Horace Mann
- *The only thing necessary for the triumph of evil is for good men to do nothing.* —Edmund Burke
- *The evil that is in the world almost always comes of ignorance, and good intentions may do as much harm as malevolence if they lack understanding.* —Albert Camus

JUNE 4

- *With colour one obtains an energy that seems to stem from witchcraft.* —Henri Matisse
- *It is easy to be wise after the event.* —English Proverb
- *The heart is wiser than the intellect.* —J. G. Holland
- *I believe that virtue shows quite as well in rags and patches as she does in purple and fine linen.* —Dickens
- *Let us not underrate the value of a fact; it will one day flower into a truth.* —Thoreau
- *I'll break my staff,*
bury it certain fathoms in the earth,
and deeper than did ever plummet sound
I'll drown my book. —Shakespeare

JUNE 5

- *A man can die but once. We owe God a death.* —Shakespeare
- *Wisdom is only found in truth.* —Goethe
- *Better a fortune in a wife than with a wife.* —Scottish Proverb
- *This is the law of God that only virtue is firm and cannot be shaken by a tempest.* —Pythagoras
- *I try to apply colours like words that shape poems like notes that shape music.* —Joan Miro
- *Each day is a little life; every waking and rising a little birth; every fresh morning a little youth; every going to rest and sleep a little death.* —Arthur Schopenhauer

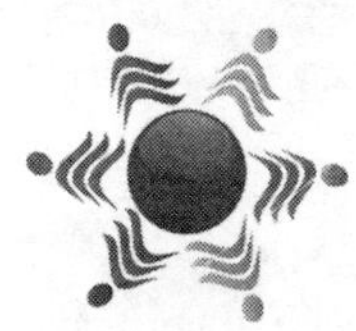

JUNE 6

- *The ability to laugh together is the essence of love.* —Francoise Sagan
- *The art of writing is the art of restraint.* —Hol. Stabbins
- *The bird a nest the a web, man friendship.* —William Blake
- *A bad workman never gets a good tool.* —Thomas Fuller
- *A covetous man's penny is a stone.* —Ali Ibu Abi Talib
- *Grow old along with me!*
  the best is yet to be,
  the last of life, for which the first was made. —Robert Browning
- *All human evil comes from this: a man's being unable to sit still in a room.* —Pascal

JUNE 7

- *A picture is a model of reality.* —Ludwig Wittgenstein
- *The price of greatness is responsibility.* —Winston Churchill
- *To err is human, to forgive, divine.* —Pope
- *No great man lives in vain. The history of the world is but the biography of great men.* —Thomas Carlyle
- *It's now the very witching time of night, when churchyards yawn and hell itself breathes out contagion to this world.* —Shakespeare

JUNE 8

- *Poets tell many lies.* —Solon
- *Man's wisdom is his best friend; folly his worst enemy.* —Sir W. Temple
- *Wisdom is the daughter of experience.* —Proverb
- *Virtue maketh men on the earth famous; in their graves illustrious; in the heavens, immortal.* —Chilo
- *Those who have great passions find themselves all their lives both happy and unhappy at being cured of them.* —La Rochefoucauld
- *I arise from dreams of thee*
  in the first sweet sleep of night
  when the winds are breathing low,
  and the stars are shining bright. — Percy

JUNE 9

- *The poet is the priest of the invisible.* —Wallace Stevens
- *Virtues all agree, but vices fight one another.* —Proverb
- *Count no man great till he is dead.* —Proverb
- *The world cannot do without great men,*
  but great men are very troublesome to the world. —Goelhe
- *Who has seen the wind?*
  Neither you nor but when the trees bow down their heads
  the wind is passing by. —Christina Rossetii

JUNE 10

- *The thing I fear most is fear.* —Montaigne
- *Nothing can be truly great which is not right.* —Samuel Johnson
- *A fool always finds one still more foolish to admire him.* —Boileau
- *A man may as well expect to grow stronger by*
  always eating as wiser by always reading. —Jerment Collier
- *Get your facts first, and then you*
  can distort them as much as you please. —Mark Twain
- *As long as there are postmen, life will have zest.* —William James
- *While we spend energy and imagination on,*
  new ways of cleaning the floors of our houses,
  the Japanese solve the problem by not dirtying them in the first place.
  —Bernard Rudofsky

JUNE 11

- *To have great poets, there must be great audiences, too.* —Walt Whitman
- *Virtue is health; vice is sickness.* —Perrarch
- *A habit is a shirt made of iron.* —Czech Proverb
- *If you wish to avoid seeing a fool,*
  you must first break your looking glass. —Rabelais
- *Drinking when we are not thirsty and making love at all seasons,*
  madam : that is an there is to distinguish us from other animals. —Pierre
- *We (Greeks) are lovers of the beautiful,*
  yet simple in our tastes, and we cultivate
  the mind without loss of manliness. —Thucydides

JUNE 12

- *Being a great writer is not the same as writing great.* —John Updike
- *He who thinks himself wise, O heavens! is a great fool.* —Voltaire
- *He is not great who is not greatly good.* —Shakespeare
- *I reject any religious doctrine that does not appeal*
  to reason and is in conflict with morality. —M. K. Gandhi
- *To be a mediocre poet, neither gods,*
  nor men, nor booksellers have allowed. —Horace
- *A man who has been the indisputable favourite of*
  his mother keeps for life the feeling of a conqueror,
  that confidence of success that often induces real success. —Freud

JUNE 13

- *To a poet nothing can be useless.* —Samuel Johnson
- *Fools rush in where angles fear to tread.* —Pope
- *Habit the shackles of the free.* —Ambrose Bierce
- *Religion a daughter of Hope and Fear, explaining to ignorance the nature of the unknowable.* —Ambrose Bierce
- *Publishing a volume of poetry is like dropping a rose petal down the or and canyon and waiting for the echo.* —Don Marquis
- *Yesterday*
  A night-gone thing
  A sun-down name. —Langston Hughes

JUNE 14

- *The greatest thing in style is to have a command, of metaphor.* —Aristotle
- *The family is more sacred than the state.* —Pope
- *Fame is proof that people are gullible.* —Ralph Waldo Emerson
- *In science, read, by preference, the newest works; in literature, the oldest. The classic literature is always modem.* —Bulwer Lytton
- *I, a stranger and afraid in a world I never made.* —A. E. Housman
- *On the road to Mandalay,*
  where the flying fishes play an' the dawn
  comes up like thunder outer China cross the Bay! —Rudyard Kipling

JUNE 15

- *A good style must, first of all, be clear. It must .. be appropriate.*

  —Aristotle
- *Greatness and goodness are not means, but ends.* —Coleridge
- *A man's best fortune or his worst, is a wife.* —Proverb
- *There is a great man who makes every man feel small.*

  But the real great man is the man who makes every man feel great.

  —Charles Dickens
- *A good style must have an ail of novelty,*

  at the same time concealing its art. —Anonymous
- *Happy he*

  with such a mother! faith in womankind

  beats with his blood. —Alfred Lord Tennyson

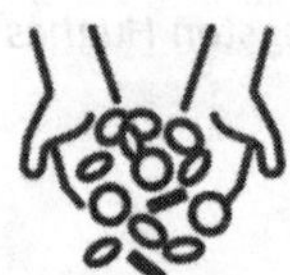

JUNE 16

- *Whatever is clearly expressed is well wrote.*

  —Lady Mary Wortley Montagu
- *War is the science of destruction.* —John S.C. Abbott
- *He that has a wife has a master.* —Scottish Proverb
- *There is no such thing as an inevitable war. If war comes,*

  it will be from failure of human wisdom. —Bonar Law
- *Chameleons feed on light and air :*

  Poets' food is love and fame. —Percy Bysshe Shelley
- *Once upon a midnight dreary, while I pondered, weak and weary,*

  over many a quaint and curious volume of forgotten lore while

  I nodded, nearly napping, suddenly there came a tapping,

  as of someone gently rapping, rapping at my chamber door.

  —Edgar Allan Poe

JUNE 17

- *This is the sort of English up with which I will not put.*
  —Winston Churchill
- *A truly great man never puts away the simplicity of a child.*
  —Chinese Proverb
- *There never was a good war or a bad peace.* —Franklin
- *Modern warfare is an intricate business about which no one knows everything and few know very much.* —Frank Knox
- *Poetry is the record of the best and happiest moments of the happiest and best minds.* —Percy Bysshe Shelley
- *There are some extraordinary fathers who seem, during the whole course of their lives, to be giving their children reasons for being consoled at their death.* —La Bruyere

JUNE 18

- *Take eloquence and wring its neck.* —Pual Vulaine
- *Habits are first cobwebs, then cables.* —Spanish Proverb
- *Genius is the father and industry the mother of greatness.* —V. Samuel
- *The opposite of love is not hate; it's indifference.* —Elie Wiesel
- *Read over your compositions, and wherever you meet with a passage which you think is particularly fine, strike It out.* —Samuel Johnson
- *This is Malaya. Everything takes a long, a very long time in Malaya. Things get done, occasionally, but more often they don't, and the more in a hurry you are, the quicker you break down.* —Han Suyin

JUNE 19

- *Style is the dress of thought.* —Samuel Wesley
- *No man is a hypocrite in his pleasures.* —Samuel Johnson
- *Hypocrisy is the homage which vice pays to virtue.* —LA Rochefqucauld
- *There never was yet philosopher*

"Well, now that we have seen each other," said the Unicorn, "if you believe in me, I' ll believe in you. Is that a bargain?" —Lewis Carroll

- *Step after step the ladder is ascended.* —George Herbert
- *"My country, right or wrong", is a thing no patriot would think of saying except in a desperate case. It is like saying, "My mother, drunk or sober".* —G.K. Chesterton

JUNE 20

- *Verbal felicity is the fruit of art and diligence and refusing to be false.* —Marianne Moore
- *She ran the whole gamut of emotions from A to B.* —Dorothy Parker
- *That could endure the toothache patiently.* —Shakespeare
- *Teach us delight in simple things, and mirth that has no bitter springs.* —Rudyard Kipling
- *For by grace are ye saved through faith; and that not of yourselves; it is the gift of God.* —Bible
- *Fear is the main source of superstition, and one of the main sources of cruelty to conquer fear is the beginning of wisdom.* —Bertrand Russell

JUNE 21

- *Of making many books, there is no end.* —Bible
- *Illness tells us what we are.* —Anonymous
- *The greatest evil is physical pain.* —ST. Augustine
- *Dear sir, your profession has, as usual, destroyed your brain.* —George Bernard Shaw
- *True wit is nature to advantage dressed, what often was thought, but never so well expressed.* —Alexander Pope
- *I have made this letter longer than usual, because I lack the time to make it short.* —Pascal

JUNE 22

- *A well written life is almost as fare as a well-spent one.* —Thomas Carlyle
- *To live by medicine is to live horribly.* —Linnaeus
- *May dear, I don't give a damn.* —Margaret Mitchell
- *I am just going to pray for you at St. Paul's, but with no very lively hope of success.* —Rev. Sydney Smith
- *Writing is nothing more than a guided dream.* —Jorge Luis Borges
- *Old age has its pleasures, which, though different, are not less than the pleasure of youth.* —W. Somerset Maugham
- *Old age has a great sense of calm and freedom. When the passions have relaxed their hold and have escaped! not from one master but from many.* —Plato

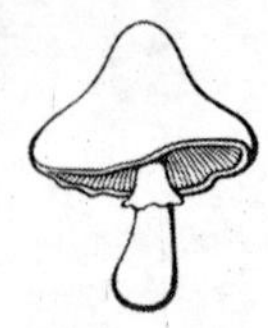

JUNE 23

- *Vigorous writing is concise.* —William Strunk
- *He wants the natural touch.* —Shakespeare
- *House beautiful is the play lousy.* —Dorothy Parker
- *It is not a novel to be thrown aside lightly. It should be thrown aside with great force.* —Dorothy Parker
- *Darling, I am growing old, silver threads among the gold.* —Eben Eugene Rexford
- *Being over seventy is like being engaged in a war. All our friends are going or gone and we survive amongst the dead and dying as on a battlefield.* —Muriel Spark

JUNE 24

- *Brevity is the soul of wit.* —Shakespeare
- *There goes the famous good time that was had by all.* —Beite Davis
- *Another damned, thick square book! Always scribble, scribble, scribble! Eh! Mr. Gibbon?* —William Henry
- *Faith in a holy cause is to a considerable extent a substitute for the lost faith in ourselves.* —Eric Hoffer
- *The wolf also shall dwell with the lamb,*
  and the leopard shall lie down with the kid;
  and the calf and the young lion and the fatling together;
  and a little child shall lead them. —Anonymous

JUNE 25

- *Proper words in proper places make the true definition of style.* —Jonathan Swift
- *Familiarity breeds contempt.* —Aesop
- *No man Is u hero to his valet.* —Anne Bigot Du Cornuel
- *If you carry with you your childhood, you never become older.* —Abraham Sutzkever
- *He that hath a wife and children hath given hostages to fortune; for they are impediments to great enterprises.* —Francis Bacon
- *Breathes there the man, with soul so dead, who never to himself has said, this is my own, my native land!* —Sir Walter Scott

JUNE 26

- *All writing comes by the grace of God.* —Ralph Waldo Emerson
- *You blocks, you stones, you worse than senseless things!* —Shakespeare
- *No matter how thin you slice it, it's still baloney.* —Alfred E. Smith
- *He never said a foolish thing nor never did a wise one.* —Earl of Rochester
- *If a writer has to rob his mother, he wlll not hcsitate; the "Ode on a Grecian Urn" is worth any number of old ladies.* —William Faulkner
- *They shall beat their swords into plowshares, and their spears into pruning hooks; nation shall not lift up sword against nation, neither shall they learn war any more.* —Bible

JUNE 27

- *As to the Adjective : when in doubt, strike it out.* —Mark Twain
- *Innocence is ashamed of nothing.* —Jean Jacques Rousseau
- *I used to be Snow White but I drifted.* —Mae West
- *The noblest prospect that a Scotchman ever sees is the high road that leads to London.* —Samuel Johnson
- *To be seventy years young is sometimes far more cheerful and hopeful than to be forty years old.* —Oliver Wendell Holmes
- *You're not supposed to be so blind with patriotism that you can't face reality. Wrong is wrong no matter who does it or who says it.* —Malcolm X

JUNE 28

- *It is with noble sentiments that bad literature gets written.* —Andre Gide
- *Innocence dwells with wisdom, but never with ignorance.* —William Blake
- *Blessed are the pure in heart : for they shall see God.* —Bible
- *Except ye be converted and become as little children, ye shall not enter into the kingdom of heaven.* —Unknown
- *Often you must turn you stylus to erase if you hope to write anything worth a second reading.* —Hohace
- *When a whole nation is roaring patriotism at the top of its voice, I am fain to explore the cleanness of its hands and purity of its heart.* —Ralph Waldo Emerson

JUNE 29

- *No man but a blockhead ever wrote, except for money.* —Samuel Johnson
- *There is less in this than meets the eye.* —Tallulah Bankhead
- *The innocent are God's elect.* —St. Clement
- *As there are misanthropists or haters of mankind, so there are mislogists or haters of ideas.* —Plato
- *A man may write at any time, if he will set himself doggedly to it.* —Samuel Johnson
- *There is not a more mean, stupid, dastardly, pitiful, selfish, spiteful, envious, ungrateful animal than the public. It is the greatest of cowards, for it is afraid of itself.* —William Hazlitt

JUNE 30

- *True ease in writing comes from art, not chance.* —Alexander Pope
- *A hypocrite is a person who ... but who isn't?* —Don Marquis
- *Being a hypocrite has marvelous advantages!* —Moliere
- *An invasion of armies can be resisted, but not an idea whose time has come.* —Victor Hugo
- *Our passions shape our books, repose writes them in the intervals.* —Marcel Proust
- *Cheat me in price, but not in the goods I purchase.* —Spanish Proverb
- *Angles fly. Because they take themselves lightly.* —G.K. Chesterton

JULY

Desire

to excel

JULY 1

- *Three hours a day will produce as much as a man ought to write.*
—Anthony Trollope
- *A nice man is man of nasty ideas.* —Jonathan Swift
- *You can't shoot an idea.* —Thomas E, Dewey
- *As for conforming outwardly,*
and living your own life inwardly, I don't think much of that.
—Thoreau
- *When everything else physical and mental seems to diminish,*
the appreciation of beauty is on the increase. —Bernard Berenson
- *Try, is a lesson you should heed,*
try, try again.
If at first you don't succeed,
try, try again. —William E. Hickson

JULY 2

- *The fool hath said in his heart, There is no God.* —Bible
- *The bottom line is in heaven.* —Edwin Herbert Land
- *Meaningless laughter is a sign of ill-breeding.* —Anonymous
- *Pray for my soul. More things are wrought by prayer*
than this world dreams of. —Alfred Lord Tennyson
- *Advice is seldom welcome and those who want it*
the most always like it the least. —Earl of Chesterfield
- *A peace is of the nature of a conquest;*
for then both parties nobly are subdued,
and neither party loser. —Shakespeare

JULY 3

- *I am an atheist still thank God.* —Luis Bunuel
- *Man thinks. God laughs.* —Jewish Proverb
- *In two words; im possible.* —Samuel Goldwyn
- *Complaint is the largest tribute heaven receives, and the sincerest part of our devotion.* —Jonathan Swift
- *The trade of advertising is now so near perfection that it is not easy to propose any improvement.* —Samuel Johnson
- *A metaphysician is a man who goes into a dark cellar at midnight without a light, looking for a black cat that is not there.* —Lord Bowen

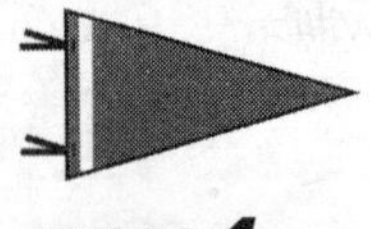

JULY 4

- *There are no atheists in the foxholes.* —William Thomas Cummings
- *A maid that laughs is half taken.* —English Proverb
- *He laughs best who laughs last.* —English Proverb
- *What is conservatism? Is it not adherence to the old and tried, against the new and untried?* —Abraham Lincoln
- *Ads push the principle of noise all the way to the plateau of persuasion. They are quite in accord with the procedures of brainwashing.* —Marshall Mcluhan
- *You may fool all the people some of the time; you can even fool some of the people all the time; but you can't fool all of the people all the time.* —Abraham Lincoln

JULY 5

- *It couldn't have happened anywhere but in little old new York.* —O. Henry
- *The tongue of man is a twisty thing.* —Homer
- *A government of laws, and not of men.* —John Adams
- *One must laugh before one is happy or one may die without ever having laughed at all.* —La Bruyere
- *Half the money I spend on advertising is wasted, and the trouble is, I don't know which half.* —John Wanamaker
- *Why should there not be a patient confidence in the ultimate justice of the people? Is there any better or equal hope in lithe world?* —Abraham Lincoln

JULY 6

- *By seeing London, I have seen as much of life as the world can show.* —Samuel Johnson
- *The people's good is the highest law.* —Cicero
- *Great cases like hard cases make bad law.* —Ouver Wendell Holmes
- *If we would guide by the light of reason, we must let our minds be bold.* —Louis D. Brandeis
- *I grow old .... I grow old .... I shall wear the bottoms of my trousers rolled.* —T.S. Eliot
- *Perseverance is more prevailing than violence; and many things which cannot be overcome when they are taken together, yield themselves up when taken little by little.* —Plutarch

JULY 7

- *Everyone soon or late comes round by Rome.* —Robert Browning
- *Law means good order.* —Aristotle
- *One law for the lion and ox is oppression.* —William Blake
- *All law has for its object to confirm and exalt into a system the exploitation of the workers by a ruling class.* —Mikhail. A. Bakunin
- *My only fear is that I may live too long. This would be a subject of dread to me.* —Thomas Jefferson
- *The more humanity owes him (the poor man), the more society denies him. Every door is shut against him, even when he has a right to its being opened; and if he ever obtains justice, it is with much greater difficulty than others obtain favors.* —Jean Jacoues Rousseau

JULY 8

- *Washington is a city of Southern efficiency and Northern charm.* —John F. Kennedy
- *Go to law for a sheep and lose your cow.* —Anonymous
- *Law is a bottomless pit.* —John Arbuthnot
- *Laugh, and the world laughs with you; weep, and you weep alone.* —Ell Wheeler Wilcox
- *Where are the songs of spring? Ay, where are they? Think not of them, thou hast thy music too ....* —John Keats
- *There is something about poverty that smells like death. Dead dreams dropping off the heart like leaves in a dry season and rotting around the feet.* —Zora Neale Hurston

JULY 9

- *Today's city is the most vulnerable social structure ever conceived by man.* —Martin Oppenheimer
- *One with the law is majority.* —Calvin Coolidge
- *Law is a horrible business.* —Clarence Darrow
- *The execution of the laws is more important than the making them.* —Thomas Jefferson
- *Match me such a marvel save in Eastern clime, a rose red city "half as old as time".* —John William burgon
- *My country has in its wisdom contrived for me the most insignificant office (the vice presidency) that ever the invention of man contrived or his imagination conceived.* —John Adams

JULY 10

- *Cities are the abyss of the human species.* —Jean Jacques Rousseau
- *Good men must not obey the laws too well.* —Ralph Waldo Emerson
- *Wife and children are bills of charges.* —Proverb
- *Life is like a box of chocolates. You never know what you're going to get.* —Forrest Gump
- *That willing suspension of disbelief for the moment, which constitutes poetic faith.* —Samuel Taylor Coleridge
- *To teach how to live without certainty and yet without being paralyzed by hesitation is perhaps the chief thing that philosophy, in our age, can do for those who study it.* —Bertrand Russell

JULY 11

- *The object of art is to give life shape.* —Jean Anouiui
- *A virtuous woman is a crown to her husband.* —Old Testament
- *The wife is the source of salvation.* —The Mahabharata
- *A great man is always willing to be little.* —Ralph Waldo Emerson
- *Iffaut epater le bourgeois. One must shock the bourgeois.* —Charles Baudelaire
- *I am more and more convinced that man is a dangerous creature and that power, whether vested in many or a few, is ever grasping, and like the grave, cries, "Give, Give".* —Abigail Adams

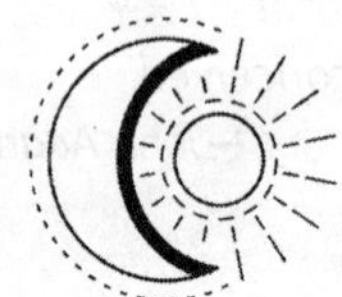

JULY 12

- *With the ancient is wisdom; and in length of days understanding*—Bible
- *Wherever law ends, tyranny begins.* —John Locke
- *A void witticisms at the expense of others.* —Horace Mann
- *Complaint is the largest tribute heaven receives, and the sincerest part of our devotion.* —Jonathan Swift
- *When a man fell into his anecdotage, it was a sign for him to retire from the world.* —Benjamin Disraeli
- *There is but one truly serious philosophical problem, and that is suicide. Judging whether life is or is not worth living amounts to answering the fundamental question of philosophy.* —Albert Camus

JULY 13

- *I have taken more good from alcohol than alcohol has taken from me.* —Winston Churchill
- *God could not be everywhere, therefore he made mothers.* —Jewish Proverb
- *Freedom is the oxygen of the soul.* —Moshe Dayan
- *The easiest way for your children to learn about money is for you not to have any.* —Katherine Whitehorn
- *Though in silence, with blighted affection, I pine, yet the lips that touch liquor must never touch mine!* —George W. Young
- *When thou prayest thou shalt not be as the hypocrites are; for they love to pray standing in the synagogues and in the corners of the streets that they may be seen of men.*
- *Verily I say unto you, they have their reward.* —Bible

JULY 14

- *I have been a stranger in a strange land.* —Bible
- *Money makes the man.* —Aristodemus
- *Old fools are more foolish than young ones.* —La Rochefoucauld
- *Money is like a sixth sense without which you cannot make a complete use of the other five.* —W. Somerset Maugham
- *Malt does more than milton can to justify God's ways to man.* —A. E. Housman
- *Power always thinks it has a great soul and vast views beyond the comprehension of the weak; and that it is doing God's service, when it is violating all His laws.* —John Adams

JULY 15

- *Successful and fortunate crime is called virtue.* —Seneca
- *The love of money is the root of all evil.* —Bible
- *There is no fool like an old fool.* —John Lyly
- *Some are born great, some achieve greatness,*
  and some have greatness thrust upon them. —Shakespeare
- *Crabbed age and youth cannot live together.*
  Youth is full of pleasance, age is full of care. —Shakespeare
- *Tench me, my God and king,*
  in dull things thee to see;
  and what I do in anything,
  to do it as for thee. —George Herbert

JULY 16

- *Expedients are for the hour, but principles are for the ages.* —Henry Ward Beecher
- *Money is like an arm or a leg-use it or lose it.* —Hemy Ford
- *Freedom cannot be granted; it must be taken.* —Max Stirner
- *Riches are not from abundance of worldly goods,*
  but from a contented mind. —Prophet Muhammad
- *Happy families are all alike;*
  every unhappy family is unhappy in its own way. —Leo Tolstoy
- *Whatever a man prays for, he prays for a miracle.*
  Every prayer reduces itself to this; "Great God,
  grant that twice two be not four". —Ivan Turgenev

JULY 17

- *As soon as one is unhappy, one becomes moral.* —Proust
- *Men are what their mothers made them.* —R.W. Emerson
- *Useless laws weaken the necessary laws.* —Montesquieu
- *Where large sums of money are concerned,*
  it is advisable to trust nobody. —Agatha Christie
- *To believe in God is to yearn for His existence,*
  and further more, it is to act as if He did exist.
  —Miguel De Vnamuno
- *You pray in your distress and in your need;*
  would that you might pray also in the fullness
  of your joy and in your days of abundance. —Kahlil Gibran

JULY 18

- *The end must justify the means.* —Matthew Prior
- *For a wife, take the daughter of a good mother.* —Thomas Fuller
- *Knowledge can be communicated but not wisdom.* —Hermann Hesse
- *They who are of opinion that money will do everything may*
  very well be suspected to do everything for money.
  —Lord Halifax
- *We live in reference to past experience and*
  not to future event, however inevitable. —H. G. Wells
- *A mind not to be changed by place or time*
  the mind is its own place, and in itself
  can make heaven of hell, a hell of Heaven.
  What matter where, if I be still the same. —John Milton

JULY 19

- *Morality is the herd instinct in the individual.* —Friedrich Nietzsche
- *What is home without a mother?* —Alice Hawthrone
- *I know but one freedom and that is the freedom of the mind.* —Antoine De Saint Exupery
- *To have enough is good luck, to have more than enough is harmful.*
  This is true of all things, but especially of money. —Chuang Tzu
- *Ring out the thousand wars of old,*
  ring in the thousand years of peace. —Alfred Lord Tennyson
- *He prayeth best, who loveth best*
  all things both great and small;
  for the dear God who loveth us
  he made and loveth all. —Anonymous

JULY 20

- *My country is the world, and my religion is to do good.* —Thomas Paine
- *Be not the slave of words.* —Thomas Carlyle
- *Man has his will but woman has her way.* —Holmes
- *War crushes, with bloody heel, all justice,*
  all happiness, all that is god-like in man. —Charles Sumner
- *Peace hath higher tests of manhood*
  than battle ever knew. —John Greenleaf whitner
- *Prayer is the little implement*
  through which men reach
  where presence is denied them. —Emily Dickinson

JULY 21

- *Rise above principle and do what's right.* —Walter Heller
- *Youth and white paper take any impression.* —English Proverb
- *The world is his who enjoys it.* —Proverb
- *Here lies my wife; here let her lie!*
  Now she's at rest, and so am I. —Dryden
- *There is always one moment in childhood*
  when the door opens and lets the future in. —Graham Greene
- *The freshness, the eternal youth,*
  of admiration sprung from truth;
  From beauty infinitely growing
  upon a mind love overflowing. —William Wordsworth

JULY 22

- *It is easier to fight for one's principles than to live up to them.* —Alfred Hitler
- *Riches serve a wise man but command a fool.* —Proverb
- *Wealth is not his that has it but his that enjoys it.* —Benjamin Franklin
- *Money is a bottomless sea, in which honour,*
  conscience and truth may be drowned. —Anonymous
- *From each according to his abilities,*
  and to each according to his needs. —Karl Marx
- *The most sublime courage I' have ever*
  witnessed has been among that class too
  poor to know they possessed it, and too
  humble for the world to discover it. —George Bernard Shaw

JULY 23

- *When I am in the country, I wish to vegetate like the country .*
  —William Hazlitt
- *Actions speak louder than words.* *—Proverb*
- *There is a woman at the beginning of all great things.* *—LA Martine*
- *In war, whichever side may call itself the victor,*
  there are no winners, but all are losers. *—Neville Chamberlain*
- *The economy of communism is an economy*
  which grows in an atmosphere of misery and want.
  —Eleanor Roosevelt
- *We don't cry for the moon*
  we pluck it from the skies
  and wear it upon the diadem
  of Asia's freedom. *—Sarojini Naidu*

JULY 24

- *Communism is the corruption of a dream of justice.* *—Adlai Stevenson*
- *A word to the wise is sufficient.* *—Terence*
- *It is good for a man that he bear the yoke in his youth.* *—Bible*
- *A mother is a mother still, the holiest thing alive.* *—Coleridge*
- *Consistency requires you to be as ignorant today as you were a year ago.* *—Bernard Berenspn*
- *Physical courage, which despises all danger,*
  will make a man brave in one way; and
  moral courage, which despises all opinion,
  will make a man brave in another. *—Colton*

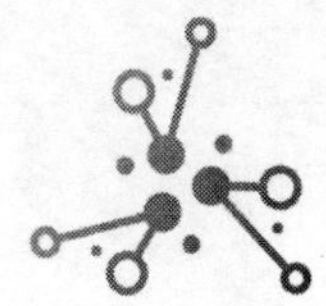

JULY 25

- *Comparisons are odious.* —John Fortescue
- *Youth and age will never agree.* —Scottish Proverb
- *But in this world nothing is sure but death and taxes.* —Franklin
- *All other goods by fortune's hand are given;*
  A wife is the peculiar gift of heaven. —Alexander Pope
- *A foolish consistency is the hobgoblin of little minds,*
  adored by little statesmen and philosophers and divines.
  —Ralph Waldo Emerson
- *The philosopher is not influenced by praise*
  or blame. He knows the truth and is not afraid,
  regardless of which happens to him in this world.
  —Taoism

JULY 26

- *Conscience is the perfect interpreter of life.* —Karl Barth
- *You can stroke people with words.* —F. Scott
- *Woman is the salvation or the destruction of the family.* —H.F. Amiel
- *In the selection of a wife as in a project of war,*
  to err but once is to be undone forever. —Middleton
- *Peace cannot be kept by force.*
  It can only be achieved by understanding. —Albert Einstein
- *Perfect courage means doing unwitnessed*
  what we would be capable of with the world
  looking at what one might be capable of
  doing before all the world. —La Rochefoucauld

JULY 27

- *Often the test of courage is not to die but to live.* —Vittorio Alfieri
- *A woman should be seen, not heard.* —Sophocles
- *Words will build no walls.* —Plutarch
- *The only comfort of my life*
  is that I never yet had wife. —Herrick
- *In the room the women come and go*
  talking of Michelangelo. —T.S. Eliot
- *We must accept life for what it actually is*
  a challenge to our quality without which we
  should never know of what stuff we are made,
  or grow to our full stature. —Virginia Hanson

JULY 28

- *I have no relish for the country; it is a kind of healthy grave* —Sydney Smith
- *Knowledge comes, but wisdom lingers.* —Tennyson
- *Wit is the salt of conversation not the food.* —William Hazlitt
- *If you can't say anything good about someone,*
  sit right here by me. —Alice Roosevelt Longworth
- *Conscience in the soul is the root of all true*
  courage. If a man would be brave, let him
  learn to obey his conscience. —Clarke

JULY 29

- *Anybody can be good in the country.* —Oscar Wilde
- *How can you write if you can't cry?* —Ring Lardner
- *Words cut more than swords.* —Proverb
- *He that loves not his wife and children, feeds a lioness at home and broods a nest of sorrows.* —Jeremy Taylor
- *The more the pleasures of the body fade away, the greater to me is the pleasure and charm of conversation.* —Plato
- *Show him the way of doing that, and the dullest day-drudge kindless into a hero. Kindle the inner genial life of him, and you have a flame that burns up all lower considerations.* —Thomas Carlyle

JULY 30

- *Only a peace between equals can last.* —Woodrow Wilson
- *All words are pegs to hang ideas on.* —Henry Ward Beecher
- *The pen is the tongue of the mind.* —Cervantes
- *It is a woman's business to get married as soon as possible, and a man's to keep unmarried as long as he can.* —George Bernard Shaw
- *Teas, where small talk dies in agonies.* —Percy Bysshe Shelley
- *Courage begets strength by struggle with hardship. Courage grows from fighting danger and overcoming obstacles. Develop the courage to act according to your convictions, to speak what is true, and to do what is right.* —Zoroastrianism

JULY 31

- *Peace is liberty in tranquillity.* —Cicero
- *Only the young die good.* —Oliver Herford
- *In the sweat of thy face shalf thou eat thy bread.* —Old Testament
- *Dig a well before you are thirsty.* —Chinese Proverb
- *Every time we read, a seed is sown for the future.* —Jules Renard
- *No bees, no honey;*
  no work, no money. —Proverb
- *I cannot hold with those who wish to put down the insignificant chatter of the world.* —Anthony Trollope
- *Eyes are more accurate witness that ears.* —Heraclitus
- *Man is born free, and everywhere he is in chain.* —Rousseau
- *Melancholy is the joy of being sad.* —Victor Hugo
- *'It's nothing for a man to hold up his head in a calm; but to maintain his post when all others have quitted their ground and there to stand upright when other men are beaten down, this is divine and praiseworthy.* —Seneca

AUGUST

Opportunity

to prove

AUGUST 1

- *Until the day of his death, no man can be sure of his courage.* —Jean Anouilh
- *All work and no play makes jack a dull boy.* —Proverb
- *If you wish to be a writer, write.* —Epictetus
- *My son's my son till he gets him a wife, my daughter's my daughter all her life.* —English Proverb
- *Courage is almost a contradiction in terms. It means a strong desire to live taking the form of a readiness to die.* —G. K. Chesterton
- *The source of courage and power is the promotion of the Word of God, and steadfastness in his love.* —Baha'i

AUGUST 2

- *Nothing is permanent except change.* —Heraclitus
- *Total absence of humour renders life impossible.* —Colette
- *A sense of humour is a sense of proportion.* —Khalil Gibran
- *The family you came from isn't as important as the family you're going to have.* —Ring Lardner
- *Fine art is that in which the hand, the head, and the heart of man go together.* —John Ruskin
- *Courage in strife is common enough; even the dogs have it. But the courage which can face the ultimate defeat of a life of good will...that is different, that is victory.* —Virginia Hanson

AUGUST 3

- *The desire for change is a sign of safety.* —John H. Patterson
- *Like mother, like daughter.* —Proverb
- *Bear and forbear.* —Epictetus
- *Knowledge is proud that he has learned so much;*
  Wisdom is humble that he knows no more. —William Cowper
- *I cannot and will not cut my conscience*
  to suit this year's fashions. —Lillian Hellman
- *Fortitude implies a firmness and strength of mind that enables us to do and suffer as we ought. It rises upon an opposition and, like a river, swells the higher for having its course stopped.*
  —Jeremy Collier

AUGUST 4

- *I want to see you shoot the way you shout.* —Theodore Roosevelt
- *As a cure for worrying, work is better than whiskey.* —Thomas A. Edison
- *He knows little who will tell his wife all he knows.* —Thomas Fuller
- *A man is in general better pleased when he has a good dinner upon table, than when his wife talks greek.*
  —Samuel Johnson
- *Conscience is the inner voice that*
  warns us somebody may be looking. —H.L. Mencken
- *The grandest of heroic deeds are those which are performed within four walls and in domestic privacy.* —Jean Paul F. Richter

AUGUST 5

- *Beauty is eternity gazing at itself in a mirror.* —Khalil Gibran
- *The essence of humour is human kindliness.* —Stephen Leacock
- *The job of satire is to frighten and enlighten.* —Richard Condon
- *Wisdom requires that we pour a little oil of delicate courtesy on the wheels of friendship.* —Colette
- *The poetical language of an age should be the current language heightened.* —Gerard Manley Hopkins
- *Courage is the red badge of our immortal spirit, who lives and grows by sacrifice and faith and love.* —Virginia Hanson

AUGUST 6

- *I tell you the past is a bucket of ashes.* —Carl Sandburg
- *One good mother is worth hundred teachers.* —English Proverb
- *No man is free who is not master of himself.* —Epictetus
- *The hand that rocks the cradle is the hand that rules the world.* —W. S. Ross
- *Abstract truth may belong to science and metaphysics, but the world of reality belongs to art.* —Rabindranath Tagore
- *The worst thing that can happen to a fighting man is to lose courage.*
Because it is not life that matters, but it is the courage that you bring to it. —Author Unknown

AUGUST 7

- *Those who cannot remember the past are condemned to repeat it.* —George Santayana
- *I think the first duty of society is justice.* —Alexander Hamilton
- *Live and let live is the rule of common justice.* —Sir Roger L Estrange
- *Judgement is not the knowledge of fundamental laws; it is knowing how to apply knowledge of them.* —Charles Gow
- *You can't change people. But you can channel them your way.* —Hal Stabbins
- *You have to believe in the heroic deeds, if you want to be a hero yourself, and mind your courage is the mettle which can transform you into one* —Mahatma Devesh Bhikshu

AUGUST 8

- *What's past is prologue.* —Shakespeare
- *A kingdom founded on injustice never lasts.* —Seneca
- *Delay of justice is injustice.* —Landor
- *Compromise makes a good umbrella but a poor roof; it is a temporary expedient.* —James Russell Lowell
- *Progress is impossible without change; and those who cannot change their minds cannot change anything.* —George Bernard Shaw
- *He either fears his fate too much,*
  or his deserts are small,
  that dares not put it to the touch,
  to gain or lose it all. —James Graham

AUGUST 9

- *Everything comes if a man will only wait.* —Benjamin Disraeli
- *Judgement is forced on us by experience.* —Johnson
- *Judge not the play before the play be done.* —John Davies
- *The man who says he is willing to meet you halfway*
  is usually a poor judge of distance. —Anonymous
- *We are inclined to believe those we do not know,*
  because they have never deceived us. —Samuel Johnson
- *Things do not change; we change.* —Thoreau
- *Not everything that is faced can be changed.*
  But nothing can be changed until it is faced. —Lewis Mumford

AUGUST 10

- *Beware the fury of a patient man.* —John Dryden
- *There is not virtue so truly great and godlike as justice.* —Joseph Addison
- *Let justice be done, though the heavens fall.* —William Watson
- *Justice should not only be done, but should manifestly and*
  undoubtedly be seen to be done. —Gordon Hewart
- *The world is weary of the past,*
  oh, might it die or rest at last. —Percy Bysshe Shelley
- *Wealth lost, something lost,*
  honor lost, much lost;

courage lost, all lost. —Johann Wolfgang Von Goethe

AUGUST 11

- *Books and friends should be few but good.* —Proverb
- *The price of justice is eternal publicity.* —Arnold Bennett
- *Help to make earth happy, like the heaven above.* —Jalia A. F. Carney
- *Justice discards party, friendship, kindred, and is always, therefore, represented as blind.* —Joseph Addison
- *Beauty is the first present Nature gives to women, and the first it takes away* —Mere
- *When moral courage feels that it is in the right there is no personal daring of which it is incapable.* —Leigh Hunt

AUGUST 12

- *He is a fine friend. He stabs you in the front.* —Leonard Louis Levinson
- *God's mill grinds slow, but sure.* —George Herbert
- *Unless justice be done to others, it will not be done to us.* —Woodrow Wilson
- *My experience has shown me that we win justice quickest by rendering justice to the other party.* —M. K. Gandhi
- *The firmest friendships have been formed in mutual adversity. Iron is most strongly willed in the fiercest flame.* —C. C. Colton
- *I wonder is it because men are cowards in heart that they admire bravery so much, and place military valor so far beyond every other quality for reward and worship.* —William Thackeray

AUGUST 13

- *Patriotism is in political life what faith is in religion.* —Lord Acton
- *Justice and mercy differ only in name.* —Swami Dayanand
- *Kindness is never wasted.* —S. H. Simmons
- *He who decides a case without hearing the other side, though he decides justly, cannot be considered just.* —Lucius Annaeus Seneca
- *All things are taken from us, and become portions and parcels of the dreadful past.* —Alfred
- *God will guide the good. Therefore they shall have no fear. He will lead them through all the rough spots of life.* —Islam

AUGUST 14

- *Patience is bitter but its fruit is sweet.* —French Proverb
- *Kindness affects more than severity.* —Aesop
- *Do not judge and you will never be mistaken.* —Rousseau
- *One cool judgement is worth a thousand hasty counsels. The thing to do is to supply light and not heat.* —Woodrow Wilson
- *Sit on the bank of a river and wait : your enemy's corpse will soon float by.* —Indian Proverb
- *Courage stands halfway between cowardice and rashness, one of which is a lack the other an excess of courage.* —Plutarch

AUGUST 15

- *The end is not yet.* —Bible
- *Kindness is that brings forth kindness always.* —Sophocles
- *Be your own judge and you will be happy.* —M. K. Gandhi
- *O judgement! thou art fled to brutish beasts, and men have lost their reason!* —Shakespeare
- *The wheel of change moves on, and those who were down go up and those who were up go down.* —Rabindranath Tagore
- *Years wrinkle the skin,*
  but to give up courage
  wrinkles the soul.

  —Samuel Ullman

AUGUST 16

- *Patience is the companion of wisdom.* —St. Augustine
- *Kind hearts are more than coronets.* —Tennyson
- *Judge not, that ye be not judged.* —Bible
- *You cannot do a kindness too soon, for you never know how soon it will be too late.* —Ralph Waldo Emerson
- *Character is a by-product; it is produced in the great manufacture of daily duty.* —Woodrow Wilson
- *Women and men of retiring timidity are cowardly only in dangers which affect themselves, but the first to rescue when others are endangered.* —Jean Paul Richte

AUGUST 17

- *Perfumes, colours and sounds echo one another.* —Charles Baudelaire
- *Knowledge comes, but wisdom lingers.* —Lord Tennyson
- *Kindness nobler ever than revenge.* —W. Shakespeare
- *Wise saying often fall on barren ground; but a kind word is never thrown away.* —Sir Arthur Helps
- *The art of progress is to preserve order amid change and to preserve change amid order.* —Alfred North Whitehead
- *Brave is he, who possessing strength displays it not, and lives in humble ways.*
- *He is brave, who fights for the downtrodden.* —Sikhism

AUGUST 18

- *Patriotism is the last refuge of a scoundrel.* —Samuel Johnson
- *Without labour nothing prospers.* —Sophocles
- *Never work without a reward, or expect a reward without work.* —Livy
- *Give every man thine ear, but few thy voice; take each man's censure, but reserve they judgement.* —Shakespeare
- *Man has a limited biological capacity for change. When this capacity is overwhelmed, the capacity is in future shock.* —Alvin Toffler
- *If we practise with the aspiration just to be in, the present moment, our lives, will gradually transform and grow wonderfully.* —Charlotte Jok Beck

AUGUST 19

- *We all of us live too much in circles.* —Disraeli
- *It is knowledge that ultimately gives salvation.* —M. K. Gandhi
- *It is easier to forgive an enemy then a friend.* —MME Dorothee Deluzy
- *Give your decision, never your reasons;*
  your decision may be right,
  your reasons are sure to be wrong. —Lord Mansfield
- *Man is so made that he can only find relaxation from*
  one kind of labour by taking up another. —Anatole France
- *When I was a young man, I vowed never to marry until*
  I found the ideal woman. Well, I found her-but alas,
  she was waiting for the ideal man. —Robert Schumann

AUGUST 20

- *To like and dislike the same things, that is, indeed, friendship.* —Catiline
- *Labour conquers all things.* —Homer
- *Knowledge is the wing wherewith we fly to heaven.* —Shakespeare
- *Knowledge is proud that he has learned so much;*
  wisdom is humble that he knows no more. —William Cowper
- *There is no such thing as a moral or an immoral book,*
  Books are well written, or badly written. —Oscar Wilde
- *Youth, youth, springtime of beauty!*
  Youth is a test of the will, a quality of imagination,
  a vigour of the emotions, a predominance of courage over timidity, of
  the appetite of adventure over love and ease. —Anonymous

AUGUST 21

- *Friendship is single soul dwelling in two bodies.* —Aristotle
- *A man's best friends are his ten fingers.* —Robert Collyer
- *One great use of words is to hide our thoughts.* —Voltaire
- *Good, to forgive; Best, to forget.* —Browning
- *Love is too young to know what conscience is;*
  Yet he who knows not conscience is shorn of love.—Shakespeare
- *The whole secret of remaining young in spite of years,*
  is to cherish enthusiasm in oneself, by poetry, by contemplation, by charity, that is by the maintenance of harmony in the soul.
  —Henri-Frederic Amiel

AUGUST 22

- *A friend is one who warns you.* —Anonymous
- *It is manlike to punish but godlike to forgive.* —Petter Von Winter
- *Laughter is the shortest distance between two people.* —Victor Borge
- *Great literature is simply language charged with*
  meaning to the utmost possible degree. —Ezra Pound
- *My youth may wear and waste,*
  but it shall never rust. —William Congreve
- *A man is still young so long as women can make him happy or unhappy. He reaches middle age when they can no longer make him unhappy. He is old when they cease to make him either happy or unhappy.* —Anon

AUGUST 23

- *God grants an easy death only to the just.* —Svetlana Aliiluyeva
- *Men... employ speech only to conceal their thoughts.* —Voltaire
- *Forgiveness adorns a soidier.* —M. K. Gandhi
- *To bring up a child in the way he should go, travel that way yourself once in a while.* —Josh Billings
- *Old men work for the span of years that still remains for them, the young work for eternity.* —jawaharlal Nehru
- *Men fear death, as children fear to go in the dark; and as that natural fear in children is increased with tales, so is the other.* —Francis Bacon

AUGUST 24

- *Be slow in choosing a friend, slower in changing.* —Benjamin Franklin
- *Music is the universal language.* —John Wilson
- *Honest labour bears a lovely face.* —Dekker
- *The happiest moments of my life have been the few which I have passed at home ill the bosom of my family.* —Jefferson
- *A state is better governed which has but few laws, and those laws strictly observed.* —Rene Descartes
- *As I approve of a youth that has something of the old man in him, so I am no less pleased with an old man that has something of the youth. He that follows this rule may be old in body, but can never be so in mind.* —Marcus Tullius Cicero

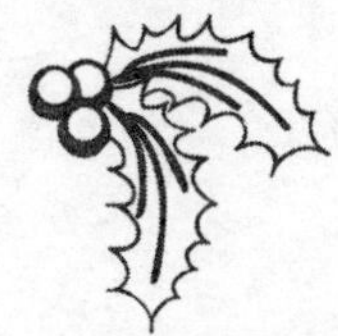

AUGUST 25

- *Chance makes our parents, but choice makes our friends.* —Delilee
- *Felicity, not fluency, of language is a merit.* —E. P. Whippe
- *Language is the dress of thought.* —Johnson
- *The sweetest sounds to mortals given*
  are heard in Mother, Home and Heaven. —W. G. Brown
- *Children are hopes. Feel the dignity of a child.*
  Do not feel superior to him, for you are not. —Robert Henri
- *I remember my youth and the feeling that will*
  never come back any more-the feeling that I could
  last forever, outlast the sea, the earth, and all men. —Joseph Conrad

AUGUST 26

- *They also serve who only stand and wait.* —John Milton
- *Laughter is a tranquillizer with no side effects.* —Arnold Glasow
- *Our sincerest laughter with some pain is fraught.* —Shelley
- *The language of the law must not be foreign to*
  the ears of those who are to obey it. —Thomas Fuller
- *Ask not what your country can do for you,*
  ask what you can do for your country. —John F. Kennedy
- *Youth can last as long as we live,*
  if we do not petrify at forty.
  A man can be bold and boy-hearted. —Herbert N. Coeson

AUGUST 27

- *The life of man is a self-evolving circle.* —Ralph Waldo Emerson
- *Nobody ever died of laughter.* —Max Beerbohm
- *Incongruity is the mainspring of laughter.* —Max Beerbohm
- *If you don't learn to laugh at trouble, you won't have any thing to laugh at when you grow old.* —Eddi Howe
- *It is one of the misfortunes of life that one must read thousands of books only to discover that one need not have read them.* —Thomas De Quincy
- *Rejoice, O young man, in thy youth; and let thy heart cheer thee in the days of thy youth, and walk in the ways of thine heart.* —Ecclesiastes

AUGUST 28

- *Christ! What are patterns for?* —Amy Lowell
- *In law nothing is certain but the expense.* —S. Butler
- *Useless laws weaken necessary ones.* —Montesquieu
- *He who has the courage to laugh is almost as much the master of the world as he who is ready to die.* —Giacomo Leopardi
- *Most women set out to try to change a man, and when they have changed him, they do not like him.* —Marlene Dietrich
- *What every young man should know is that financial success depends on two things; brains and hard work. Sometimes a little bit of luck helps.* —William Feather

AUGUST 29

- *The wheel is come full circle.* —Shakespeare
- *Nothing is more silly than silly laughter.* —Catullus
- *Laws grind the poor, and rich men rule the law.* —Goldsmith
- *I like the laughter that opens the lips and the heart,*
  that shows at the same time pearls and the soul. —Victor Hugo
- *Patriotism is a kind of religion; it is the egg*
  from which wars are hatched. —Guy De Maupassant
- *How beautiful is youth! How bright it gleams*
  with its illusion, aspirations, dreams!
  Book of Beginnings, story without End,
  each maid a heroine, and each man a friend!
  —Henry Wadsworth Longfellow

AUGUST 30

- *Peace, like charity, begins at home.* —Franklin Delano Roosevelt
- *History is the essence of innumerable biographies.* —Thomas Carlyle
- *Great is the force of habit; it teaches us to bear labour and to scorn injury and pain.* —Cicero
- *Children are like wet cement. Whatever falls on them makes an impression.* —Haim Ginott
- *Nobody grows old by merely living a number of years;*
  people grow old only by deserting their ideals;
  years wrinkle the skin, but to give up enthusiasm wrinkle the soul.
  —Unknown

AUGUST 31

- *It is fear that first brought gods into the world.* —Petronius
- *Habit is a great deadner.* —Samuel Beckett
- *The best secret of happiness is renunciation.* —Andrew Carnegie
- *The greater the number of laws, the greater the number of offenses against them.* —Havelock Ellis
- *What government is the best? That which teaches us to govern ourselves.* —Goethe
- *You are as young as your faith, as your self-confidence, and as your hope. So long as your heart receives messages of beauty, cheer, courage, grandeur and power from the earth, from man and from the infinite, so long you are young.* —Author Unknown
- *Excess on occasion is exhilarating. It prevents moderation from acquiring the deadening effect of habit:* —W. Somerset Maugham
- *Hate is the subtlest form of violence.* —M.K. Gandhi
- *The ability to laugh together is the essence of love.* —Francoise Sagan

Promise

to excellence

SEPTEMBER 1

- *They make a desert and call it peace.* —Tacitijs
- *Habit is ten times nature.* —Wellington
- *The fox changes his skin but not his habits.* —Suetonius
- *The history of the world is the record of a man in quest of his daily bread and butter.* —H.W. Van Loon
- *He who would pass the declining years of his life with honour and comfort, should, when young, consider that he may one day become old, and remember, when he is old, that he has once been young.* —Joseph Addison

SEPTEMBER 2

- *The most disadvantageous peace is better than the most just war.* —Erasmus
- *Man is the artificer of his own happiness.* —Thoreau
- *One joy scatters a hundred griefs.* —Chinese Proverb
- *I have learned to seek my happiness by limiting my desires, rather than in attempting to satisfy them.* —John Stuart Mill
- *There is nothıng so strange and so unbelievuble lhul it has not been said by one philosopher or another.* —Rene Descartes
- *The young and old have all answers. Those in between are stuck with the questions. In youth we run into difficulties, in old age difficulties run into us.* —Josh Billing

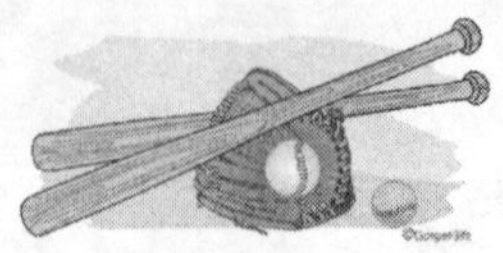

SEPTEMBER 3

- *Where law ends, there tyranny begins.* —William Pitt
- *Hate is a prolonged form of suicide.* —Douglas Steere
- *It is easy to hate but it is healthy to love.* —S. Radhakrishnan
- *He who sees Him in all and all in Him, hates none.*
  He who feels for others as he feels for himself, loves all.
  —Ishopanishad
- *The test of a religion or philosophy is*
  the number of things it can explain. —Ralph Waldo Emerson
- *Innocent youth is a priceless possession not*
  to be squandered away for the sake of a
  momentary excitement miscalled pleasure. —Mahatma Gandhi

SEPTEMBER 4

- *What would youth be without love?* —George Gordon Byron
- *History is only a confused heap of facts.* —Earl of Chesterfield
- *Early to bed and early to rise,*
  makes a man healthy, wealthy and wise. —Benjamin Franklin
- *What is to be a philosopher?*
  Is it not to be prepared against events? —Epictetus
- *In youth, we clothe ourselves with rainbows,*
  and go as brave as the zodiac. In age, we put
  out another sort of perspiration, gout, fever,
  rheumatism, caprice, doubt, fretting, avarice.
  —Ralph Waldo Emerson

SEPTEMBER 5

- *Youth supposes; age knows.* —Proverb
- *History repeats itself.* —Proverb
- *Health is the vital principal of bliss.* —J. Thomson
- *Happiness is a Swedish sunset-it is there for all,*
  but most of us look the other way and lose it. —Mark Twain
- *You cannot do without philosophy,*
  since everything has its hidden meaning which we must know.
  —Maxim Gorky
- *Let us live then; and be glad*
  while young life's before us
  After youthful pastime had,
  after old age hard and sad,
  Earth will slumber over us. —John Addington Symonds

SEPTEMBER 6

- *Kindnesses, likes grain, increases by sowing.* —Proverb
- *He laughs best who laughs last.* —English Proverb
- *Ill habits gather by unseen degrees.*
  As brooks make rivers run into seas. —Dryden
- *Do not all charms fly*
  youth is the time to go flashing from one end of
  the world to the other both in mind and body;
  to try the manners of different nations;
  to hear the chimes at midnight. —Robert Louis Stevenson

SEPTEMBER 7

- *Logic is the art of making truth prevail.* —La Bruyere Les
- *All living faith is acquired and not inherited.* —Nirad C. Chaudhury
- *Politics are not the task of a Christian.* —Dietrich Bonhoeffer
- *There is nothing which strengthens faith more than the observance of morality.* —Addison
- *Metaphysics is almost always an attempt to prove*
  the incredible by an appeal to the unintelligible. —H.L. Mencken
- *When two men shake hands and part,*
  mark which of the two takes the sunny side (of the street):
  he will be the younger man of the two. —E.C. Bulwer-Lytton

SEPTEMBER 8

- *If youth be a defect, it is one that we outgrow only too soon.* —James Russell Lowell
- *Faith is the root of all blessings.* —Jeremy Taylor
- *Politics ruins the character.* —Otto Von Bismarck
- *We hate some persons because we do not know them;*
  and we will not know them because we hate them. —C.C. Colton
- *Most philosophical treatises show the human*
  cerebrum loaded far beyond its plimsoll mark. —H. L. Mencken
- *Gone are the games of childhood,*
  and gone forever is youth,
  and gone is the world that was kind of us,
  and love, and faith, and truth. —Heinrich Heine

SEPTEMBER 9

- *To philosophize is to doubt.* —Mont Aigne
- *History is a set of lies agreed upon.* —Napoleon Bonaparte
- *Man prefers to believe what he prefers to be true.* —Francis Bacon
- *Faith does not depend upon experience; it is somethinq that is there before experience.* —Shri Aurobindo
- *Wonder is the foundation of all philosophy, inquiry the process ignorance the end.* —Unknown
- *Society must alternate between revolution and consolidation. It is the function of youth to supply this dynamic element.* —Jawaharlal Nehru

SEPTEMBER 10

- *Faith knows no disappointment.* —M.K. Gandhi
- *Health and cheerfulness mutually beget each other.* —Addison
- *The heart of the fools is in his mouth, but the mouth of the wise man is in his heart.* —Benjamin Franklin
- *Anger is short madness, so control your passion or it will control you.* —Horace
- *The man who gets angry at the right things and with the right people, and in the right way and at the right time and for the right length of time, is commended.* —Aristotle

SEPTEMBER 11

- *An angry man opens his mouth and shuts up his eyes.* —Cato
- *Finality is not the language of politics.* —Benjamin Disraeli
- *A burnt child dreads the fire.* —English Proverb
- *I have but one lamp by which my feet are guided, and that is the lamp of experience.* —Patrie Henry
- *From tavern to tavern youth dances along*
  with an arm full of girl and a heart full of song.
  —Author Unidentified
- *Youth is a blunder,*
  manhood a struggle,
  old age a regret. —Benjamin Disraeli

SEPTEMBER 12

- *Never answer a letter while you are angry.* —Chinese Proverb
- *Faith is continuation of reason.* —William Adams
- *Hatred is the madness of the heart.* —Lord Byron
- *Experience is a jewel, and it had need to be so,*
  for it is often purchased at an infinite rate.
  —William Shakespeare
- *The charities that soothe, and heal, and bless,*
  lie scattered at the feet of men like flowers. —Wordsworth
- *Youth though it may lack knowledge,*
  is certainly not devoid of intelligence;
  it sees through shams with sharp and terrible eyes. —Henry Louis Mencken

SEPTEMBER 13

- *Beware the fury of a patient man.* —Dryden
- *The worst hatred is that of relatives.* —P.C. Tactitus
- *A sound mind in a sound body.* —Greek Proverb
- *Men are wise in proportion, not to their experience,*
  but to their capacity for experience. —George Bernard Shaw
- *Wonder is the feeling of a philosopher,*
  and philosophy begins in wonder, —Plato
- *In the lexicon of youth,*
  which fate reserves
  For a bright manhood,
  there is no such word as fail. —Bulwer-Lytton

SEPTEMBER 14

- *Anger raises invention, but it overheats the oven.* —Lord Halifax
- *Success goes to your head, failure to your heart.* —Anonymous
- *If you have faith in the cause and the means and in God,*
  the hot sun will be cool for you. —M.K. Gandhi
- *Philosophy arises from an unusually obstinate attempt to*
  arrive at real knowledge. —Bertrand Russell
- *I don't believe one grows older. I think that*
  what happens early on in life is that at
  a certain age, one stands still and stagnates. —T.S. Eliot

SEPTEMBER 15

- *Politics is a blood sport.* —Aneurin Bevan
- *Knowledge is power.* —Hobbes
- *Hatred is self punishment.* —Housaballon
- *The great question is not whether you have failed, but whether you are content with failure.* —Anonymous
- *There are more things in heaven and earth, Horatio, than are dreamt of in your philosophy.* —Shakespeare
- *When I was a young man I vowed never to marry until I found the ideal woman. Well, I found her-but alas, she was waiting for the ideal man.* —Robert Schumann

SEPTEMBER 16

- *We walk by faith, not by sight.* —New Testament
- *Faith means belief in something concerning which doubt is theoretically possible.* —William James
- *Childhood and genius have the same master-organ in common-inquisitiveness.* —E.G. Bulwer Lytton
- *While thou are young thou will think it will never have an end but the longest day have its evening, and thou shall enjoy it but once; it never turns again use it therefore as the spring-time, which soon departeth, and wherein thou oughtest to plane and show all provisions for a long and happy life.*

—Sir Walter Raleigh

SEPTEMBER 17

- *The unexamined life is not worth living.* —Socrates
- *Experience is the best teacher.* —Proverb
- *Faith is the force of life.* —Tolstoy
- *There's only one thing more painful than learning from experience, and that is not learning from experience.* —Anonymous
- *You have all the characteristics of a popular politician: horrible voice, bad breeding, and a vulgar manner.* —Aristophanes
- *As I approve of a youth that has something of the old man in him, so I am no less pleased with an old man that has something of the youth. He that follows this rule may be old in body, but can never be so in mind.* —Marcus Tullius Cicero

SEPTEMBER 18

- *Man is by nature a political animal.* —Aristotle
- *Knowledge without practice makes but half an artist.* —Proverb
- *There is no fiercer hell than failure in a great object.* —John Keats
- *Failure is more frequently from frequently from want of energy than want of capital.* —Daniel Webster
- *We know what happens to people who stay in the middle of the road. They get run over.* —Aneurin Bevan
- *The whole secret of remaining young in spite of years, is to cherish enthusiasm in oneself, by poetry, by contemplation, by charity, that is by the maintenance of harmony in the soul.* —Henri-Frederic Amiel

SEPTEMBER 19

- *Certain peace is better than anticipated victory.* —Livy
- *Either do not attempt at au or go through with it.* —Ovid
- *Let no one be willing to speak ill of the absent.* —Propertius
- *Talking and eloquence are not the same: to speak, and to speak well, are two different things.* —Ben Jonson
- *Politics is the art of the possible,*
  the attainable ..., the art of the next best. —Otto Von Bismarck
- *Our youth began with tears and sighs,*
  with seeking what we could not find;
  We sought and knew not what we sought;
  We marvel, now we look behind:
  Life's more amusing that we thought. —Andrew Lang

SEPTEMBER 20

- *Political action is the highest responsibility of a citizen.* —John F. Kennedy
- *History is mostly guessing; the rest is prejudice.* —Will and Ariel Durant
- *Happiness lies, first of all, in health.* —George William Curts
- *Sometimes a noble failure serves the world as faithfully*
  as a distinguished success. —Dowden
- *Politicians are the same all over.*
  They promise to build bridges, even where there are no rivers. —Nikita Khrushchev
- *If you judge people, you have no time to love them.* —Mother Teresa

SEPTEMBER 21

- *All reactionaries are paper tigers.* —Mao Tse-Tung
- *History is philosophy teaching by examples.* —Dionysius of Halicarnassus
- *An intellectual hatred is the worst.* —W.B. Yeats
- *Failure is often God's own tool for carving some of the finest outlines in the character of his children.* —T. Hodgkin
- *Liberal institutions straightway cease from being liberal the moment they are soundly established.* —Friedrich Nietzsche
- *Youth can last as long as we live, if we do not petrify at forty. A man can be bold and boy-hearted.* —Herbert N. Coeson

SEPTEMBER 22

- *The only alternative to co-existence is co-destruction.* —Jawaharlal Nehru
- *Where all men think alike, no one thinks very much.* —Walter Lippmann
- *Hear much; Speak litle.* —Bias
- *The first wealth is health.* —R. W. Emerson
- *Age considers, youth ventures.* —Anonymous
- *Truth is strengthened by observation and delay; falsehood by haste and uncertainty.* —Tacitus
- *It isn't enough to talk about peace. One must believe in the people's voice is odd, it is, and is not, the voice of God.* —Imitations of Horace

SEPTEMBER 23

- *Who builds upon the people, builds upon sand.* —Italian Proverb
- *One good schoolmaster is worth a thousand priests.* —Robert G. Ingersoll
- *The art of teaching is the art of assisting discovery.* —Mark Van Doren
- *Tear's are the safety valves of the heart when too much pressure is laid on it.* —A. Smith
- *Old wood best to burn, old wine to drink, old friends to trust and old authors to read.* —Bacon
- *Youth is a test of the will, a quality of imagination, a vigour of the emotions, a predominance of courage over timidity, of the appetite of adventure over love and ease.* —Anonymous

SEPTEMBER 24

- *Politics is not an exact science.* —Otto Von Bismarck
- *Great thoughts come from the heart.* —Vauvenargues
- *Who hath none to still him, may weep out his eyes.* —Proverb
- *Heavy hearts, like heavy clouds in the sky, are best relieved by the letting of water.* —Rivarol
- *Experience is good if not bought too dear.* —Proverb
- *The first forty years of life give us the text; the next thirty supply the commentary on it.* —Schopenhauer
- *I remember my youth and the feeling that will never come back any more-the feeling that I could last forever, outlast the sea, the earth, and all men.* —Joseph Conard

SEPTEMBER 25

- *To be angry is to revenge the faults of others on ourselves.* —Pope
- *Learning without thought is labour lost.* —Confucius
- *The mind grows by what it feeds on.* —J. G. Holland
- *People should think things out fresh and not just accept conventional terms and the conventional way to doing things.* —Buckminster Fuller
- *The old believe everything; the middle-aged suspect everything; the young know everything.* —Wilde

SEPTEMBER 26

- *An old man is twice a child.* —Shakespeare
- *Truth makes the devil blush.* —Proverb
- *A stitch in time saves nine.* —English Proverb
- *To climb steep hills requires slow pace at first.* —Shakespeare
- *A man that is young in years may be old in hours, if he had lost no time.* —Francis Bacon
- *I am getting old and the sign of old age is that I begin to philosophize and ponder over problems which should not be my concern at all.* —Jawaharlal Nehru
- *Some books are to be tasted, others to be swallowed, and some few to be chewed and digested.* —Francis Bacon
- *Adversity's sweet milk, philosophy.* —Shakespeare

SEPTEMBER 27

- *The most precious things in speech are the pauses.* —Ralph Richardson
- *Teaching others teacheth yourself.* —Proverb
- *Tears are the silent language of grief.* —Voltaire
- *Words may be false and full of art,*
  sighs are natural language of the heart. —Thomas Shadwell
- *A man is as old as he's feeling,*
  a woman as old as she looks. —Mortimer Collins
- *Sing like no one's listening, love like you've never been hurt,*
  dance like nobody's watching and
  live like it's heaven on Earth. —Mark Twain

SEPTEMBER 28

- *In teaching there should be no class, distinctions.* —Confucius
- *Time is a rat that cuts the thread of life.* —Swami Sivananda
- *The busy have no time for tears.* —Byron
- *Blessed is the man who, having nothing to say,*
  abstains from giving us wordy evidence of the fact. —George Eliot
- *A diplomat is a man who always remembers a woman's*
  birthday but never remembers her age. —Robert Frost
- *Hatred is blind, as well as love.* —Thomas Fuller
- *You are as young as your faith, as your self-confidence,*
  and as your hope. So long as your heart receives messages
  of beauty, cheer, courage, grandeur and power from the earth,
  from man and from the infinite, so long you are young.
  —Author Unknown

SEPTEMBER 29

- *Philosophy will dip an angers wing.* —John Keats
- *Save your breath to cool your porridge.* —Proverb
- *Tears are summer showers to the soul.* —Alfred Austin
- *To be good is noble,but to teach others how to be good is nobler and less trouble.* —Mark Twain
- *Whenever a man's friends begin to compliment him about looking young, he may be sure that they think he is growing old.* —Washington Irving
- *Nobody grows old by merely living a number of years; people grow old only of deserting their ideals; years wrinkle the skin, but to give up enthusiasm wrinkle the soul.* —Unknown

SEPTEMBER 30

- *I only ask to be free. The butterflies are free.* —Charles Dickens
- *Speech is of time; silence is of eternity.* —Thomas Carlyle
- *An age builds up cities : an hour destroys them.* —Seneca
- *Lose an hour in the morning and you will be looking for it in the rest of the day.* —Lord Chestelfield
- *One should never trust a woman who tells one her real age. A woman who would tell one that, would tell one anything.* —Oscar Wilde
- *From birth to age eighteen, a girl needs good parents. From eighteen to thirty-five, she needs good looks. From thirty-five to fifty-five, she needs a good personality. From fifty-five on, she needs good cash.* —Sophie Tucker

OCTOBER

Believe

the dedication

OCTOBER 1

- *The people want to be deceived.* —Roman Epigraph
- *Truths and roses have thorns about them.* —Proverb
- *Make use of time, let not advantage slip.* —Shakespeare
- *The object of teaching a child is to enable him to get along without his teacher.* —Elbert Hubbard
- *In the common people there is no wisdom, no penetration, no power of judgement.* —Cicero
- *The young and old have all answers.*
  Those in between are stuck, with the questions.
  In youth we run into difficulties,
  in old age difficulties run into us. —Josh Billings

OCTOBER 2

- *Anger blows out the lamp of the mind.* —Ingersoll
- *Nobody becomes guilty by fate.* —Seneca
- *And that is not happiness.* —F.H. Braoley
- *But to him who tries and fails and dies, I give great honour and glory and tears.* —Joaquin Miller
- *There is a myth that government can do the job cheaply because it doesn't have to make a profit.* —E. S. Savas
- *Let us live then; and a glad*
  while young life's before us.
  After youthful pastime had,
  after old age hard and sad,
  Earth will slumber over us. —John Addington Symonds

OCTOBER 3

- *The form of government is unimportant.*
  What is important is its spirit. —General Schmidt
- *The lady doth protest too much, methinks.* —Shakespeare
- *Be virtuous and you will be eccentric.* —Mark Twain
- *Nothing has an uglier look to us than reason,*
  when it is not on our side. —Lord Halifax
- *If it has to choose who is to be crucified,*
  the crowd will always save Barabbas. —Jean Cocteau
- *In youth, we clothe ourselves with rainbows,*
  and go as brave as the zodiac. In age, we put
  out another sort of perspiration, gout, fever,
  rheumatism, caprice, doubt, fretting, avarice.
  —Ralph Waldo Emerson

OCTOBER 4

- *All the world over, I will back the masses against the classes.*
  —William Gladstone
- *Habit, if not resisted, soon becomes necessity.* —St. Augustine
- *The greatest virtue of man is perhaps curiosity.* —Anatole France
- *He who will not reason is a bigot; he who cannot is a fool;*
  and he who dares not is a slave. —Sir William Dqimmond
- *Nor is the people's judgement always true;*
  The most may err as grossly as the few. —John Dryden

OCTOBER 5

- *The wealth of a country is its working people.* —Theodor Herzl
- *Make us happy and you make us good.* —Robert Browning
- *Virtue is learned at the mother's knee; vice at other joints.*—Anonymous
- *Whenever one finds oneself inclined to bitterness, it is a sign of emotional failure.* —Bertrand Russell
- *The great masses of the people will more easily fall victims to a big lie than to a small one.* —Adolf Hitler
- *Innocent youth is a priceless possession not to be squandered away for the sake of a momentary excitement miscalled pleasure.* —Mahatma Gandhi

OCTOBER 6

- *The people are a many-headed beast.* —Horacer
- *Nine-tenths of wisdom consists in being wise in time.* —T. Roosevelt
- *How beautiful is victory, but how dear!* —Boufflers
- *The last function of reason is to recognize that there is an infinity of things which surpass it.* —Pascal
- *Death is not the greatest loss in life. The greatest loss is what dies inside us while we live.* —Norman Cousins
- *Youth is the time to go flashing from one end of the world to the other both in mind and body; to try the manners of different nations; to hear the chimes at midnight.* —Robert Louis Stevenson

OCTOBER 7

- *The people are the only sure reliance for the preservation of our liberty.* —Thomas Jefferson
- *Tearless grief bleeds inwardly.* —Bovee
- *He who seeks truth should belong to no country.* —Voltaire
- *If I had to choose a religion, the sun as the universal giver of life would be my god.* —Napoleon Bonaparte
- *About things on which the public thinks long, it commonly thinks right.* —Samuel Johnson
- *I don't believe one grows older. I think that what happens early on in life is that at a certain age, one stands still and stagnates.* —T.S. Eliot

OCTOBER 8

- *Every man a king!* —Huey Long
- *Winning isn't everything, but wanting to win is* —Vince lombardi
- *Religion is the last refuge of human savagery.* —Alfred North
- *Who overcomes by force hath overcome but half his foe.* —John Milton
- *The people, and the people alone, are the motive force in the making of world history.* —Mao Tse—Tung
- *Youth, though it may lack knowledge, is certainly not devoid of intelligence; it sees through shams with sharp and terrible eyes.* —Henry Louis Mencken

OCTOBER 9

- *Slow and steady wins the race.* —Aesop
- *'Tis' virtue, and not birth, that makes us noble.* —John Fletcher
- *A good wife and health is a man's best wealth.* —Proverb
- *Men will wrangle for religion; write for it; fight for it; die for it; anything but-live for it* —Charles Caleb Colton
- *I am the people the mob-the crowd-the mass. Do you know that all the great work of the world is done through me?* —Carl Sandburg
- *When two men shake hands and part, mark which of the two takes the sunny side (of the street): he will be the younger man of the two.* —E.C. Bulwer-Lytton

OCTOBER 10

- *He that can't endure the bad will not live to see the good.* —Jewish Proverb
- *For beauty's tears are lovelier than her smile.* —Campbell
- *Never return hatred for hatred, nor injury for injury.* —Lord Krishna
- *I learned to work in the mornings, when I could skim the cream off the day and then use the rest for cheese-making.* —J.W. Goethe
- *Let me make the newspapers, and I care not what is preached on the pulpit or what is enacted in Congress.* —Wendell Phillips
- *Society must alternate between revolution and consolidation. It is the function of youth to supply this dynamic element.* —Jawaharlal Nehru

OCTOBER 11

- *He that endureth to the end shall be saved.* —Bible
- *I wasted time and now doth time waste me.* —Shakespeare
- *Love is loviest when embalmed in tears.* —Walter Scott
- *In teaching, it is the method and not the content that is the massage... the drawing out, not the pumping in.* —Ashley Montagu
- *The dull period in the life of an event is when it ceases to be news and has not begun to be history.* —T. Hardy
- *The only thing necessary for the triumph of evil is for good men to do nothing.* —Edmund Burke

OCTOBER 12

- *Be there a win and wisdom finds a way.* —George Crabbe
- *Do not squander time for that is the stuff life is made of.* —Franklin
- *Those tender tears always humanize the soul.* —Thomson
- *Half the spiritual difficulties that men and women suffer arise from a morbid state of health.* —H. W. Beecher
- *To persevere, trusting in what hopes he has, is courage in a man. The coward despairs.* —Euripides
- *We design our lives through the power of choices.* —Richard Bach

OCTOBER 13

- *Much effort, much prosperity.* —Euripides
- *If folly were grief, every house would weep.* —Proverb
- *Hatred is like fire; it makes even light rubbish deadly.* —George Eliot
- *Speech without the backinq of experience based on action will lack chastity and refinement.* —M. K. Gandhi
- *The bird of time has but a little way to flutter-and the bird is on the wing.* —Omar
- *There is a feeling of eternity in youth which makes amends for everything. To be young is to be as one of the immortals.* —William Hazlitt

OCTOBER 14

- *There is nothing so ridiculous but some philosopher has said it.* —Cicero
- *Nothing is harder on your laurels than resting on them.* —Franklin Jones
- *Truth sits upon the lips of dying men.* —Matthew Arnold
- *You cannot teach a man anything; you can only help him to find it within himself.* —Gaweo
- *The ruler proclaims the good news himself; he sends the servants out to announce the bad news.* —Serbian Proverb
- *Yes, you may depend upon it, he has the ability! He is the younger generation that stands ready to knock at my door to make an end of Halvard Solness.* —Henrick Ibsen

OCTOBER 15

- *God helps those who persevere.* —Koran
- *History is only interesting as long as it is strictly true.* —Lord David Cecil
- *The will of the people is the best law.* —Ulysses S. Grant
- *Exercise is bunk. If you are healthy, yo don't need it; if you are sick, you shouldn't take it.* —Henry Ford
- *Sorrow and silence are strong, and patient endurance is godlike.* —Henry Wadsworth Longfellow
- *Knowing yourself is the beginning of all wisdom.* —Aristotle

OCTOBER 16

- *Great works are performed not by strength, but by perseverance.* —Samuel Johnson
- *Truth is no road to fortune.* —Rousseau
- *A law is not a law without coercion behind it.* —Jemes A. Gardield
- *In history, characters and events occur twice first as tragedy, then as farce.* —Karl Marx
- *Endurance is the crowning quality, and patience all the passion of great hearts.* —James Russell Lowell
- *The men and women who are old but mentally young are the wisest people in any country, and we should rely on them for leadership.* —Unknown

OCTOBER 17

- *A politician... one that would circumvent God.* —Shakespeare
- *Speech is the gift of all, but the thought of few.* —Anonymous
- *Successful minds work like a gimlet to a single point.* —Bovee
- *A teacher who is attempting to teach without inspiring the pupil with a desire to learn is hammering on cold iron.* —Horace Mann
- *It is now known... that men enter local politics solely as a result of being unhappily married.* —Cyril Northcote Parkinson
- *The morning time is a fox, the evening a wolf. In youth we are beguiled by time, in old age we are devoured by it.* —Unknown

OCTOBER 18

- *All politics are based on the indifference of the majority.* —James Reston
- *There is no new thing under the sun.* —Bible
- *Nothing quite new is perfect.* —Cicero
- *Go and catch a falling star, get a child with mandrake root.* —John Donne
- *Double, double toil and trouble, fire burn and caldron bubble.* —Shakespeare
- *There is nothing in the world so demoralizing as money.* —Unknown
- *Youth is not a time of life. It is not a matter of pink cheeks and supple limbs. It is a state of mind. We are as young as our self-confidence; as old as our fear.* —Unknown

OCTOBER 19

- *A reactionary is a somnambulist walking backward.* —Anonymous
- *Only the past, when you were happy, is real.* —Anonymous
- *In the carriages of the past you can't go anywhere.* —Maxim Gorky
- *Children begin by loving their parents. After a time they judge them. Rarefy, if ever, do they forgive them.* —Oscar Wilde
- *He knows nothing and thinks he knows everything. That points clearly to a political career.* —George Bernard Shaw
- *Be it a weakness, it deserves some praise,*
  we love the play-place of our early days;
  The scene is touching, and the heart is stone,
  that feels not at that sight, and feels at home. —William Cowper

OCTOBER 20

- *Nothing is more foreign to us Christians than politics.* —Tertullian
- *Wind of the western sea.* —Alfred, Lord Tennyson
- *It ain't a fit night out for man or beast.* —W. C. Fields
- *Of one power even God is deprived, and that is the power of making what is past never to have been.* —Agathon
- *Politics is perhaps the only profession for which no preparation is thought necessary.* —Robert Louis Stevenson
- *Take her up tenderly*
  lift her with care
  fashioned so slenderly
  young, and so fair. —Thomas Hood

OCTOBER 21

- *The poor man's wisdom is despised and his words are not heard.*

—Bible

- *Obedience is in a way the mother of all virtues.* —St. Augustine
- *Nevertheless, not my will, but thine, be done.* —Bible
- *Now the New Year reviving old desires,*
  the thoughtful Solitude retires. —Edward Fitzgerald
- *In politics, if you want anything said, ask a man;*
  if you want anything done, ask a woman.

—Margaret Thatcher

- *Remember now thy creator in the days of thy youth,*
  while the evil days come not, nor the years draw night.
  when thou shalt say, I have no pleasure in them. —Ecclesiastes

OCTOBER 22

- *A party is perpetually corrupted by personality.* —Ralph Waldo Emerson
- *Learn to obey before you command.* —Solon
- *The past is the present. Isn't it? It's the future too.* —Eugene Oneill
- *The constellations were consulted for advice,*
  but no one understood them. —Elias Canetti
- *Politics is not the art of the possible.*
  It consists in choosing between the disastrous and the unpalatable.

—John Kenneth Galbraith

- *Youth loves honor and victory more than money.*
  It really cares next to nothing about money,
  for it has not yet learned what the lack of if means. —Aristotle

OCTOBER 23

▪ *Life is not a problem to be solved, but a reality to be experienced.*

—Soren Kierkegaard

▪ *The question is not who is going to let me;*
It's who is going to stop me. —Ayn Rand

▪ *Those who make you believe absurdities can make you commit atrocities.* —Voltaire

▪ *Once you've accepted your flaws, no one can use them against you.*

—George R.R. Martin

▪ *When we strive to become better than we are, everything around us becomes better too.* —Paolo

▪ *Our greatest fear should not be of failure ...but of succeeding at things in life that don't really matter.* —George Eliot

OCTOBER 24

▪ *Challenges are what make life interesting and overcoming them is what makes life meaningful.* —Joshua J. Marine

▪ *You will face many defeats in life, but never let yourself be defeated.*

—Maya Angelou

▪ *Keep your face to sunshine and you can never see the shadow.*

—Helen Keller

▪ *Always forgive your enemies; nothing annoys them so much.*

—Oscar Wilde

▪ *Do not go where the path may lead; go instead where there is no path and leave a trail.* —Ralph Waldo Emerson

▪ *If life were predictable it would cease to be life and be without flavor.*

—Eleanor Roosevelt

▪ *Tell me and I forget. Teach me and I remember. Involve me and I learn.*

—Benjamin Franklin

OCTOBER 25

- *Youth is quick in temper but weak in judgement.* —Homer
- *The fog come in to on little cat feet.* —Carl Sandburg
- *Night, when words fade and things come alive.*
  —Antoine De Saint-Exupery
- *Sweet and low, sweet and low,*
  is not the night mournful, sad, and melancholy? —Rebelais
- *Philosophy begin in wonder, and at the end,*
  when philosophic thought has done its best, the wonder remains.
  —Alfred North Whitehead
- *Youth is a fast gallop over a smooth track to the*
  bright horizon... The time of great expectations for
  yourself and expectations of others for you-to be
  fulfilled at an unspecified time called "Someday".
  —Harold Azine

OCTOBER 26

- *Philosophy is not a body of doctrine but an activity.*
  —Ludwig Wittgenstein
- *Let them obey that know not how to rule.* —Shakespeare
- *Night hath a thousand eyes.* —John Lyly
- *Thank heaven, the sun has gone in,*
  and I don't have to go out and enjoy it. —Logan Pearsall Smith
- *The smiles, the tears of boyhood's years,*
  the words of love then spoken. —Thomas Moore
- *Most propositions and questions that have been*
  written about philosophical matters are not false but senseless.
  —Anonymous
- *Young is an inside matter. Your body grows old,*
  but your body is not you. We do not count a man's years,
  until he has nothing else to count. —Ralph Waldo Emerson

OCTOBER 27

- *Better of live in peace than to begin a war and lie dead.* —Chief Joseph
- *Obedience is a hard profession.* —Pierre Corneille
- *It is much safer to obey than to rule.* —Thomas A Kempis
- *It is right that what is just should be obeyed;*
  it is necessary that what is strongest should be obeyed.
  —Pascal
- *First keep peace within yourself,*
  then you can also bring peace to others. —Thomas A Kempis
- *We think our fathers fools,*
  so wise we grow;
  Our wiser sons, no doubt,
  will think us so. —Alexander Pope

OCTOBER 28

- *Youth will have his course.* —John Lyly
- *Nothing hurts worse than the loss of money.* —Livy
- *All wealth is the product of labour.* —John Locke
- *What's a thousand dollars? Mere chicken feed.*
  A poultry matter. —Groucho Marx
- *There are few sorrows, however poignant,*
  in which a good income is of no avail, —Logan Pearsall Smith
- *Youth is the first victim of war; the first fruit*
  of peace. It takes 20 years or more of peace
  to make a man; it takes only 20 seconds of war to destroy him.
  —Baudouin

OCTOBER 29

- *It is fatal to enter any war without the will to win it.*

  —Douglas Mac Arthur
- *You can never be too skinny or too rich.* —Barbara "Babe" Paley
- *The rich have many consolations.* —Plato
- *The dark night of the soul through which the soul*
  passes : on its way to the Divine Light. —St. John of the Cross
- *Peace hath her victories*
  no less renowned than war. —John Milton
- *What a young man has written is always*
  best enjoyed by young people.

Even if the world progresses generally,
youth will always begin at the beginning.

—Johann Wolfgang Von Goethe

OCTOBER 30

- *For the poor always ye have with you.* —Bible
- *Life is a god's novel. Let him write it.* —Issac Bashevis Singer
- *For money you would sell your soul.* —Sophocles
- *Money is like a sixth sense without which you*
  cannot make a complete use of the other five.

  —W. Somerset Maugham
- *Your old men shall dream dreams,*
  your young men shall see visions. —Joel
- *Never mistake motion for action.* —Ernest Hemingway

OCTOBER 31

- *Sweet are the uses of adversity;*
  which, like the toad, ugly and venomous,
  wears yet a precious jewel in his head;
  and this our life, exempt from public haunt,
  finds tongues in trees, books in the running brooks,
  sermons in stones, and good in everything.

  —*William Shakespeare*
- *'It's said that some have died for love.* —*William Wordsworth*
- *Love is blind.* —*Geoffrey Chaucer*
- *We are always getting ready to five but never living.*

  —*Ralph Waldo Emerson*

NOVEMBER

Identity

to courage

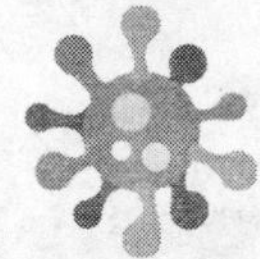

NOVEMBER 1

- *Poverty makes you sad as well as wise.* —Bertolt Brecht
- *Lack of money is the root of all evil.* —George Bernard Shaw
- *The tears of an heir are masked laughter.* —Publilius Syrus
- *My heart's in the Highlands, my heart is not here,*
  my heart's in the Highlands a-chasing the deer. —Robert Burns
- *When a dog bites a man that is not news,*
  but when a man bites a dog that is news. —John B. Bogart
- *Young men are fitter to invent than to judge;*
  fitter for execution than for counsel;
  and fitter for new projects than for settled business. —Francis Bacon

NOVEMBER 2

- *Eats first, morals after.* —Anonymous
- *I fear the Greeks even when they bring gifts.* —Virgil
- *Neither a borrower nor a lender be.* —Shakespeare
- *The more mysterious, the more imperfect; that which is*
  mystically woken is but half spoken. —Benjamin Wiuchcote
- *If you want to know what God thinks of money,*
  look at the people he gives it to. —Anonymous
- *Some young men are in such a hurry to*
  become complete adults that they get rid of
  any sign of youthfulness. And not until late in
  life do they realise that this was a mistake. —Herbert N. Casson

NOVEMBER 3

- *Poverty demoralizes.* —Ralph Waldo Emerson
- *I'm troubled, I'm dissatisfied. I'm Irish.* —Marianne Moore
- *The Japanese have perfected good manners and made them indistinguishable from rudeness.* —Paul Theroux
- *Nature never did betray the heart that loved her.* —William Wordsworth
- *The old believe everything : The middle-aged suspect everything : the young know everything.* —Oscar Wilde

NOVEMBER 4

- *A decent provision for the poor is the true test of civilisation.* —Samuel Johnson
- *All those men have their price.* —Sir Robert Walpole
- *Money should circulate like rainwater.* —Thornton Wilder
- *How can you be expected to govern a country that has two hundred and fortysix kinds of cheese?* —Charles De Gaulle
- *A man who both spends and saves money is the happiest man, because he has both enjoyments.* —Samuel Johnson
- *Denunciation of the young is a necessary part of the hygiene of older people and greatly assists in the circulation of their blood.* —Logan Pearall Smith

NOVEMBER 5

- *A man who has nothing can whistle in a robber's face.* —Juvenal
- *It is the source of all true art and science.* —Albert Einstein
- *There is no death. Only a change of worlds.* —Seattle
- *The hand that rules the press, the radio, the screen,
and the far-spread magazine rules the country.* —Learned Hand
- *Love in a hut, with water and a crust,
is love, forgive us-cinders, ashes, dust.* —John Keats
- *What every young man should know is that
financial success depends on two things :
brains and hard work. Sometimes a little bit of luck helps.*
—William Feather

NOVEMBER 6

- *Anticipate charity by preventing poverty.* —Maimonides
- *The medium is the message.* —Marshall Mcluhan
- *Now Barabbas was a publisher.* —Lord Byron
- *It is not enough to cater to the nation's
whims - you must also serve the nation's needs.* —Anonymous
- *If a free society cannot help the many who are poor,
it cannot save the few who are rich.* —John F. Kennedy
- *When the waitress puts the dinner on the table,
the old men look at the dinner.
The young men look at the waitress.* —Gelett Burgess

NOVEMBER 7

- *The greatest of evils and the worst of crimes is poverty.*
  —George Bernard Shaw
- *Without mysticism man call achieve nothing great.* —Andre Gide
- *That man is the richest whose pleasures are the cheapest.* —Thoreau
- *The new electronic interdependence re-creates the world in the image of a global village.* —Marshall Mcluhan
- *I have been a common man and a poor man; and it has no romance for me.* —Anonymous
- *What we do on some great occasion will probably on what we already are; and what we are will be the result of previous years of self-discipline.* —H.P. Liddon

NOVEMBER 8

- *A hungry man is not a free man.* —Adlai Stevenson
- *Television is a form of soliloquy.* —Sir Kenneth
- *The only sin is mediocrity.* —Martha Graham
- *If there is anything disagreeable going on, men are sure to get out of it.* —Jane Austen
- *Poverty is no disgrace to a man, but it is profoundly inconvenient.* —Reverend Sydney Smith
- *No man, who continues to add something to the material, intellectual and moral well-being of the place in which he lives, is left long without proper reward.* —Booker T. Washington

NOVEMBER 9

- *No one can worship God or love his neighbour on an empty stomach.*

—Woodrow Wilson

- *A man in the house is worth two in the street.* —Mae West
- *Memory is the treasury and guardian of all things.* —Cicero
- *Don't talk to me about naval tradition,*
  It's nothing but rum, sodomy and the lash. —Winston Churchill
- *In these days we fight for our ideas;*
  and newspapers are our fortresses. —Heine
- *Every human being has to work to carry on within,*
  duties to perform abroad, influence to exert, which are peculiarly his, and which no conscience but his own can teach.

—William Ellery Channing

NOVEMBER 10

- *A friend in power is a friend lost.* —Henry Brooks Adams
- *A large army is always disorderly.* —Euripide
- *One's prime is elusive.* —Muriel Spark
- *If it moves, salute it. If it doesn't move,*
  pick it up. If you can't pick it up, paint it. —Anonymous
- *Power tends to corrupt and absolute power corrupts*
  absolutely ... Great men are almost always bad men.

—Lord Acton

- *Youth is not a time of life. It is not a matter of pink cheeks and supple limbs.*
  It is a state of mind. We are as young as our self-confidence; as old as our fear. —Unknown

NOVEMBER 11

- *There is no power but of God.* —Bible
- *The paragon of animals!* —Shakespeare
- *Memory is the mother of all wisdom.* —Aeschylus
- *Some memories are realities, and are better than anything that can ever happen to one again.*—Willa Cather
- *Originality consists in thinking for yourself, and not in thinking unlike other people.* —Sir Fitziames Stephen
- *How do we spend our old age? In defending opinions, not because we believe them to be true, but simply because we once said that we thought they were.* —G.C. Lichtenberg

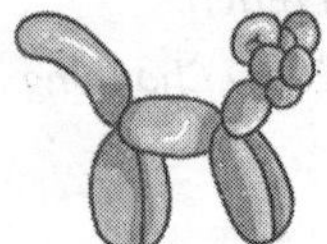

NOVEMBER 12

- *The greater the power, the more dangerous the abuse.* —Edmund Burke
- *A man is a god in mins.* —Ralph Waldo Emerson
- *Every man has a wild animal in him.* —Frederick, The Great
- *There are certain things in which mediocrity is insupportable-poetry, music, painting, public speaking.* —La Bruyere
- *The man who never alters his opinion is like standing water, and breeds reptiles of the mind.* —Blake
- *Few people are capable of expressing with equanimity opinions which differ from the prejudices of their social environment. Most people are even incapable of forming such opinions.*—Albert Einstein
- *Intelligence forbids tears.* —Doris Lessing

NOVEMBER 13

- *It's a bad plan that can't be changed.* —Publilius Syrus
- *The people are like water and the army is like fish.* —Mao Tse-Tung
- *Every man over forty is a scoundrel.* —George Bernard Shaw
- *The services in wartime are fit only for desperadoes, but in peace are fit only for fools.* —Benjamin Disraeli
- *Politics, as a practice, whatever its professions, has always been the systematic organisations of hatreds.* —Henry Brooks Adams
- *So nigh is grandeur to our dust,*
  so near is God to man.
  When Duty whispers low, 'Thos must',
  the youth replies, 'I can'. —Ralph Waldo Emerson

NOVEMBER 14

- *A liberal is a man who tells other people how to spend their money.* —Anonymous
- *God is always on the side of the big battalions.* —Marshalurenne
- *An army marches on its stomach.* —Napoleon Bonaparte
- *There's nothing so stubborn as a man when you want him to do something.* —Jean Giraudoux
- *Politics is the art of preventing people from taking part in affairs which properly concern them.* —Paul Valery
- *Mere longevity is a good thing for those who*
  watch life the side lines.
  For those who play the game, an hour may be a year,
  a single day's work an achievement for eternity. —Gabriel Heatter

NOVEMBER 15

- *You and me, we've made a separate peace.* —Ernest Hemingway
- *The rich and powerful know he is.* —Jean Anouilh
- *A rich man's joke is always funny.* —Thomas E. Browne
- *The British soldier can stand up to anything except the British War Office.* —Anonymous
- *Never lose your temper with the press or the public is a major rule of political life.* —Christabel Pankhurst
- *Determination and discipline can be learnt from ants. They are, perhaps, the most determined, hard-working and orderly creatures, living on this earth. Man would do well to emulate them.* —Anonymous

NOVEMBER 16

- *All power, of whatever sort, is desirable.* —Samuel Johnson
- *Ready money is Aladdin's lamp.* —Lord Byron
- *Youth is useless to a poor man.* —Sanskrit Proverb
- *Stick close to your desks and never go to sea,*
  and you all may be Rulers of the Queen's Navee! —W.S. Gilbert
- *Originality, I fear, is too often only undetected*
  and frequently unconsicous plagiarism. —W. R. Inge
- *You are never too old to set another goal or*
  to dream a new dream. —G.S. Lewis

NOVEMBER 17

- *Power is the great aphrodisiac.* —Henry Kissinger
- *He has an old mind in a young body.* —Eschylus
- *Youth comes but once in a lifetime.* —Henry Wadsworth Longfellow
- *The century on which we are entering can be and must be the century of the common man.*—Henry A. Wallace
- *It is hard to fail, but is worse never to have tried to succeed. In this life we get nothing save by effort.* —Theodore Roosevelt
- *The only method by which people can be supported is out of the effort of those who are earning their own way. We must not create a deterrent to hard work.* —Robert

NOVEMBER 18

- *Power never takes a back step - only in the face of more power.* —Malcolm X
- *Youth must store up; age must use.* —Seneca
- *The fewer his years, the fewer his tears.* —H.G. Bohn
- *Cannon to right of them cannon to left of them, cannon behind them. Volleyed and thundered.* —Anonymous
- *Every communist must grasp the truth; political power grows out of the barrel of a gun.* —Mao Tse Tung
- *God be thanked, the meanest of His creatures boasts two soul-side one to face the world with, one to show a woman when he loves her.* —Robert Browning

NOVEMBER 19

- *What would youth be without love?* —George Gordon Byron
- *Whoever is happy will make others happy to.* —Anne Frank
- *Anger is one of the sinews of the soul.* —Thomas Fuller
- *Youth changes its tastes by the warmth of its blood, age retains its tastes by habit.* —La Rochefoucauld
- *Political power is merely the organized power of one class to oppress another.* —Karl Marx and Friedrich Engels
- *When you loved me, I gave you the whole sun and stares to play with. I gave you eternity in a single moment, strength of the mountains in one clasp of your arms, and the volume of all the seas in one impulse of your soul.* —G. Bernard Shaw

NOVEMBER 20

- *We cannot all the masters.* —Shakespeare
- *I came, I saw, I conquered.* —J. Caesar
- *It is the beginning of the end.* —Talleyrand
- *Gentlemen, we are being killed on the beaches. Let's go inland and be killed.* —General Norman Cota
- *Power, like a desolating pestilence, pollutes whatever it touches.* —Percy Bysshe Shelley
- *First time he kissed me, he but kissed the fingers of this hand whence with I write and ever since, it grew more clear and white.* —Elizabeth Barrett Browning

NOVEMBER 21

- *Power takes as ingratitude the writhing of its victims.*

  —Rabindranath Tagore
- *Being and thought are one.* —Jean Dubuffet
- *What once was thought can never be undone.* —Friedrich Dorrenmatt
- *Theirs is not to reason why, theirs is but to do and die.* —Alfred
- *On earth there is nothing great but man;*
  in man there is nothing great but mind. —Sir William Hamilton
- *The angel that presided o'er my birth*
  said, Little Creature, formed of joy and Mirth,
  go love without the help of anything on Earth. —William Blake

NOVEMBER 22

- *Ask the gods nothing excessive.* —Aeschylus
- *Money is the wise man's religion.* —Euripides
- *Sighted sub, sank same.* —Donald F. Mason
- *The strength of an army lies in strict discipline*
  and undeviating obedience to its officers. —Thucydides
- *It is in vain to expect our prayers to be heard,*
  if we do not strive as well as pray. —Aesop
- *Little boy kneels at the foot of the bed,*
  droops on the little hands little gold head.
  Hush; Hush; Whisper who dares;
  christopher Robin is saying his prayers. —A.A. Milne

NOVEMBER 23

- *To pray is to work, to work is to pray.* —Benedictine Order
- *All the modem inconveniences.* —Mark Twain
- *The love of money is the root of all evil.* —Bible
- *My center is giving way, my right is in retreat;*
  situation excellent. I am attacking. —Ferdinand Foch
- *The feeble tremble before opinion, the foolish defy it,*
  the wise judge it, skilful direct it. —MME Jeanne Roland
- *Above all, we cannot afford not to live in the present.*
  He is blessed over all mortals who loses no moment
  of the passing life in remembering the past. —Henry David Thoreau

NOVEMBER 24

- *The wish to pray is a prayer in itself.* —Georges Bernanos
- *Imagination is more important than knowledge.* —Albert Einstein
- *Reason can wrestle and overthrow terror.* —Euripibes
- *A youth to whom was given*
  so much of earth, so much of heaven. —William Wordsworth
- *God is in heaven, and thou upon earth;*
  Therefore let thy words be few. —Bible
- *How do I love thee? Let me count the ways,*
  I love thee to the depth and breadth and height
  My soul can reach, when feeling out of sight
  for the ends of being and ideal Grace.

  —Elizabeth Barrett Browning

NOVEMBER 25

- *Politics makes strange bedfellows.* —Charles Dudley Warner
- *The sins of youth are paid for in old age.* —Latin Proverb
- *Money disappears like magic.* —Arab Proverb
- *Every man thinks! God is on his side.*
  Money is far more persuasive than logical arguments.
  —Euripides
- *Some praise at morning what they blame at night, but always think the last opinion right.* —Alexander Pope
- *All is not lost; the unconquerable will,*
  and study of revenge, immortal hate.
  And courage never to submit or yield,
  and what is else not to be overcome. —John Milton

NOVEMBER 26

- *Hunger knows no friend but its feeder.* —Aristophanes
- *Meditation is not a means to an end.*
  It is both the means and the end. —Krishnamurti
- *There is no greater sorrow than to recall,*
  in misery, the time when we were happy. —Dante
- *I say man has ever yet been half devout enough,*
  none has ever yet adored or worship'd half enough,
  none has begun to think how divine he himself is, and
  how certain the future is. —Walt Whitman

NOVEMBER 27

- *Poverty is the parent of revolution and crime.* —Aristotle
- *At some disputed barricade.* —Alan Seeger
- *Sooner or later, false thinking brings wrong conduct.* —Julian Huxley
- *Youth is a fire, and the years are a pack of wolves who grow bolder as the fire dies down.* —Unknown
- *In our time, political speech and writing are largely the defense of the indefensible.* —George Orwell
- *I always love to begin a journey on Sundays because I shall have the prayer of the Church, to preserve all that travel by land or by water.* —Jonathan Swift

NOVEMBER 28

- *Watch and pray.* —Bible
- *Both were young, and one was beautiful.* —George Gordon Byron
- *He wears the rose of youth upon him.* —William Shakespeare
- *Ah, take the Cash, and let the Credit go, nor heed the rumble of a distant Drum.* —Edward Fitzgerald
- *Prayer indeed is good, but while calling on the gods, a man should himself lend a hand.* —Hippocrates
- *Let not one look of fortune cast you down;*
  she were not fortune, if she did not frown;
  Such as do braveliest bear her scorn awhile
  are those on whom at last, she most will smile. —John Boyle
- *Youth passes as quickly as thought.* —Theognis

NOVEMBER 29

- *Prayer is conversation with God.* —Clement of Alexandria
- *There are times when even justice brings harm with it.* —Sophocles
- *Justice is the crowning glory of the virtues.* —Cicero
- *The old age of an eagle is better than the youth of a sparrow.* —Proverb
- *There are few men who would dare publish to the world the prayers they make to almighty God.* —Montaigne
- *Tradition and patriotism are a call to man's higher feelings, to something beyond his own immediate self. Love of country breeds service.* —Ronald Cartland

NOVEMBER 30

- *And fools, who came to scoff, remained to pray.* —Oliver Goldsmith
- *Justice is truth in action.* —Benjamin Disraeli
- *Christ is God clothed with human nature.* —Benjamin Whichcote
- *In youth we believe many things that are not true; in old age we doubt many truths.* —Proverb
- *His worst fault is that he is given to prayer. He is something peevish that way.* —Shakespeare
- *And yet I wish but for the thing I have;*
  My bounty is as boundless as the sea,
  my love as deep, the more I give to thee,
  the more I have, for both are infinite. —Romeo and Julit

DECEMBER

Revolution

to freedom

DECEMBER 1

- *Love truth, but pardon error.* —Voltaire
- *A fox should not be of the jury at a goose's trial.* —Thomas Fuller
- *Justice consists in ting from no man what is his.* —Thomas Hobbes
- *Loyalty to petrified opinion never yet broke a chain or freed a human soul.* —Mark Twain
- *In every age, the vilest specimens of human nature are to be found among demagogues.* —Thomas Macaulay
- *Love is a flame which burns in heaven,*
  and whose soft reflections radiate to us;
  two world are opened, two
  live gives to it; it is by love that we double our being;
  It is by love that we approach God. —Aime-Martin

DECEMBER 2

- *Everything changes but change.* —Zangwill
- *It is a wise father that knows his own child.* —Shakespeare
- *Who doesn't desire his father's death?* —Fedor Dostoevski
- *All women become like their mothers. That is their tragedy. No man does. That's his.* —R Wilde
- *Politics is war without bloodshed, while war is politics with bloodshed.* —Mao Tse-Tung
- *In this brief life the memory of one hour*
  of perfect love is worth all the joys,
  and he who has it not, though he be king,
  goes beggared through the world. —Ella Wheeler Wilcox

DECEMBER 3

- *Man is what he believes.* —Anton Chekhov
- *Be ye therefore wise as serpents and harmless as doves.* —Anonymous
- *Astrology is framed by the devil.* —Martin Luther
- *Man lives freely only by his readiness to die, if need be,*
- *at the hands of his brother, never by killing him.* —M.K. Gandhi
- *As it was in the beginning, is now, and ever shall be;*
  world without end. A man. —Book of Common Prayer
- *There is so much good in the worst of us,*
  and so much bad in the best of us,
  that it hardly becomes any of us
  to talk about the rest of us. —E.W. Hoch

DECEMBER 4

- *Dream as if you'll live forever.*
  Live as if you'll die today. —James Dean
- *Pacifism is simply undisguised cowardice.* —Adolf Hitler
- *He that spareth his rod hateth his son.* —Bible
- *Non-violence is the first article of my faith.*
  It is also the last article of my creed. —M.K. Gandhi
- *Let us be thankful for the fools.*
  But for them the rest of us could not succeed. —Mark Twain
- *Would that the little flowers were born tc live,*
  conscious of half the pleasure which they give;
  that to this mountain daisy's sell were known
  the beauty of its star-shaped showed, thrown
  on the smooth surface of this naked stone. —William Wordsworth

DECEMBER 5

- *Sweet mercy is nobility's true badge.* —Shakespeare
- *Honor thy father and thy mother.* —Bible
- *To fear the worst oft cures the worse.* —Shakespeare
- *The mysterious East, perfumed like a flower,*
  silent like death, dark like a grave. —Joseph Conrad
- *Better to hunt in fields for health unbought than*
  fee the doctor for nauseous draught. —Dryden
- *The secret of a good memory is attention,*
  and attention to a subject depends upon our interest in it.
- *We rarely forget that which has made a deep impression on our minds.*
  —Tryon Edwards

DECEMBER 6

- *It is by forgiving that one is forgiven.* —Mother Teresa
- *Ireland is the old sow that eats her farrow.* —James Joyce
- *I believe the power to make money is a gift of God.* —John D. Rockefeiller
- *People are always rather bored with their parents.*
  That's human nature. —W. Somerset Maugham
- *God gives us the courage to stand for*
  something lest we fall for anything. —Peter Marshall
- *Deep peace of the Running Wave to you.*
  Deep peace of the Flowing Air to you

Deep peace of the Quiet Earth to you.
Deep peace of the shining Stars to you.
Deep peace of the Sun of Peace to you. —Celtic Benediction

DECEMBER 7

- *Love truth, but pardon error.* —Voltaire
- *Glory be to God for dappled things.* —Gerard Manley Hopkins
- *The world is charged with the grandeur of God.*—Gerard Manley Hopkins
- *How sharper than a serpent's tooth it is*
  to have a thankless child! —Shakespeare
- *I know that love makes all things equal : I have heard*
  by mine own heart this joyous truth averred.
  The spirit of the worm beneath the sod,
  in love and worship, blends itself with God. —P.B. Shelley

DECEMBER 8

- *Blessed are the merciful : for they shall obtain mercy.* —Bible
- *One touch of nature makes the whole world kin.* —Shakespeare
- *The poetry of earth is never dead.* —John Keats
- *Nature goes her own way, and all that to us seems an*
  exception is really according to order. —Goethe
- *The condition upon which God has*
  given liberty to man is eternal vigilance. —John Philpot Curran
- *Be thou a bring flame before me,*
  be thou a guiding star above me,
  be thou a smooth path below me,
  be thou a kindly shepherd behind me,
  today-tonight-and forever. —Saint Columba of Iona

DECEMBER 9

- *I only ask to be free. The butterflies are free.* —Charles Dickens
- *Great loves too must be endured.* —Coco Chanel
- *Necessity knows no law.* —Publilius Syrus
- *No man is above the law and no man is below it;*
  nor do we ask any man's permission when we require him to obey it.
  —Theodore Roosevelt
- *People who take time to be alone usually have depth,*
  originality, and quiet reserve. —John Miller
- *Live while you live, the epicure would say,*
  and seize the pleasures of the present day;
- *Live while you live, the sacred preacher cries,*
  and give to God each moment as it flies.

Lord, in pleasure when I live to thee. —Phillip Dodridge

DECEMBER 10

- *To err is human, to forgive, divine.* —Alexander Pope
- *Love is a product of habit.* —Lucretius
- *Delicacy is to love what grace is to beauty.* —Madame De Maintenon
- *Man's love is of man's life a thing apart,*
  it's woman's whole existence. —Lord Byron
- *Every human being is intended to have a character of his own;*
  to be what no others are, and to do what no others can do.
  —William Ellery Chahning
- *Love rules the court, the camp, the grove,*
  and men below, and saints above;

for love is Heaven, and Heaven is Love. —Sir Walter Scott

DECEMBER 11

- *There can be no real freedom without the freedom to fail.* —Eric Hoffer
- *It is impossible to love and be wise.* —Francis Bacon
- *Life imitates art far more than art imitates life.* —Oscar Wilde
- *For heaven be thanked, we live in such an age,*
  when no man dies for love, but on the stage. —John Dryden
- *Many ideas grow better when transplanted into*
  another mind than in the one where they sprang up.
  —Oliver Wendell Holmes
- *That a man, I throw, is doubly curst,*
  who of the best doth make the worst;

And he I'm sure is doubly blest,
who of the worst can make the best;
To sit and sorrow and complain,
is adding folly to our pain. —William Combe

DECEMBER 12

- *What stands if freedom fall?* —Rudyard Kipling
- *There must be more to life than having everything!* —Maurice Sendak
- *Life is just one damn thing after another.* —Elbert Hubbard
- *For Satan finds some mischief still for idle hand to do.* —Isaac Watts
- *The quality of mercy is not strained,*
  it droppeth as the gentle rain from heaven. —Shakespeare
- *We know not life's reason, the*
  length of its season,

know not if they know, the great ones above.
We none of us sought it,
and few could support it,
were it not gilt with the glamour of Love. —The Garden of Karma

DECEMBER 13

- *No beast so fierce but knows some touch of pity.* —Shakespeare
- *All mankind love a lover.* —Ralph Waldo Emerson
- *Laziness is often mistaken for patience.* —French Proverb
- *Love, all alike, no season knows, nor clime,*
  nor hours, days, months, which are the rags of time.
  —John Donne
- *Courage is a good word. It has a ring. It is a substance that other people, who have none, urge you to have when all is lost. To have courage, one must first be afraid. The deeper the fear, the more difficult the climb toward courage.* —Jim Bishop

DECEMBER 14

- *Those who deny freedom to others, deserve it not for themselves.*
  —Abraham Lincoln
- *As love's young dream.* —Thomas Moore
- *Love is a kind of warfare.* —Ovid
- *Two souls with but a single thought, two hearts that beat as one.*
  —Maria Lovell
- *Originality is the fine art of remembering what you hear but forgetting where you heard it.* —Anonymous

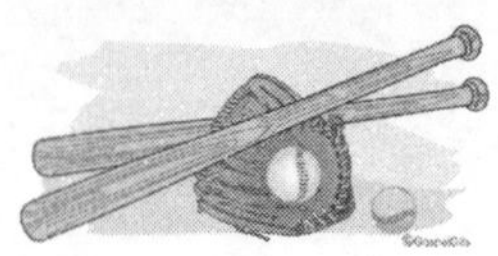

DECEMBER 15

- *License they mean when they cry liberty.* —John Milton
- *She who has never loved has never lived.* —John Gay
- *It's love that makes the world go round!* —W.S. Gilbert
- *If one judges love by the majority of its effects, it is more like hatred than friendship.* —La Rochefoucauld
- *A nation may lose its liberties in a day, and not miss them for a century.* —Montesquieu
- *As courage and intelligence are the two qualifications best worth a good man's cultivation, so it is the first part of intelligence to recognize our precarious estate in life, and the first part of courage to be not at all abashed before the fact.* —R.L. Stevenson

DECEMBER 16

- *Liberty is the right to do everything which the laws allow.* —Anonymous
- *But love is blind, and lovers cannot see the pretty follies that themselves commit.* —Shakespeare
- *Those men and women are fortunate who are born at a time when a great struggle for human freedom is in progress.* —Emmeline Pankhurst
- *Our ability to do is in accordance with our courage and confidence. We have strength in proportion to that courage. Let us, therefore, learn first courage which is but a state of mind, and we shall be able to accomplish the seemingly impossible.* —Author Unknown

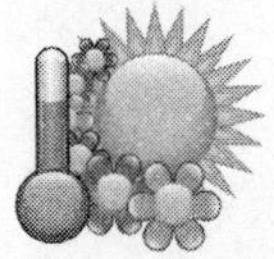

DECEMBER 17

- *O liberty, O liberty, what crimes are committed ill your name.*
  —Madame Roland
- *Than never to have loved at all.* —Alfred Lord Tennyson
- *Speak low, if you speak love.* —Shakespeare
- *How good is man's life, the mere living! how fit to employ*
  all the heart and the soul and the sense for ever in joy!
  —Anonymous
- *Courage is the standing army of the soul*
  which keeps it from conquest, pillage and slavery.
  —Henry Van Dyke
- *We look forward to a world founded upon four essential*
  freedoms (freedom of speech, freedom of worship, freedom
  from want, freedom from fear). —Franklin Delano Roosevelt

DECEMBER 18

- *Man is condemned to be free.* —Jean-Paul Sartre
- *Love knows nothing of order.* —St. Jerome
- *Life is an abnormal business.* —Eugene Ionesco
- *Carelessness about our security is dangerous, carelessness*
  about our freedom is also dangerous. —Adlai Stevenson
- *No need of looking behind,*
  forward! we want infinite energy,
  infinite zeal, infinite courage
  and infinite patience,
  then only will great things be achieved. —Swami Vivekananda

DECEMBER 19

- *Caged birds accept each other but flight is what they long for.*

—Tennessee Williams

- *Love teaches even asses to dance.* —French Proverb
- *The heart that loves is always young.* —Greek Proverb
- *There is no disguise which can hide love for long where it exists, or simulate it where it does not.*

—Anonymous

- *Some people's idea of (free speech) is that they are free to say what they like, but if anyone says anything back, that is an outrage.* —Winston Churchill
- *If every daily task be faced with courage and unflinchingly the very consciousness that we are doing our best, makes the difficulty small and the task less toilsome.*

—Author Unknown

DECEMBER 20

- *In a free state there must be free speech.* —Domitian
- *Life consists in what a man is thinking of all day.* —Anonymous
- *Oh, the wild joys of living!* —Robert Browning
- *Love is a familiar. Love is a devil. There is no evil angel but Love.* —Shakespeare
- *Let reason be opposed to reason, and argument to argument, and every good government will be safe.* —Thomas Erskine
- *You can only protect your liberties in this world by protecting the other man's freedom. You can only be free if I am freed.* —Clarence Darrow

DECEMBER 21

- *Character is a long-standing habit.* —Plutarch
- *Love means never having to say you're sorry.* —Erich Segal
- *All the world' a stage,*
  and all the men and women merely players. —Shakespeare
- *The most stringent protection of free speech would not*
  protect a man from falsely shouting
  fire in a theater and causing a panic. —Gliver Wendell Holmes
- *A man may conquer thousands and*
  thousands of invincible foes but that is of no
  real consequence; his greatest victory is when
  he conquers only his own self through indomitable courage.

—Jainism

DECEMBER 22

- *Everything flows and nothing stays.* —Heraclitus
- *The mass of men lead lives of quiet desperation.* —Thoreau
- *We are easily duped by those we love.* —Moliere
- *Life is short, art long, opportunity fleeting, experience*
  treacherous, judgement difficult. —Hippocrates
- *I disapprove of what you say,*
  but I will defend to the death your right to say it. —Voltaire
- *The course of true love never did run smooth.* —Shakespeare

DECEMBER 23

- *Change yourself if you wish to change the world.* —The Mother
- *Old and young, we are all on our last cruise.* —Robert Louis Stevenson
- *While there's life, there's hope.* —Terence
- *Men have died from time to time and worms have eaten them, but not for love.* —Shakespeare
- *One friend in a life is much, two are many, three are hardly possible.* —Henry Brooks Adams
- *One impulse from a vernal wood*
  may teach you more of man,
  of moral evil and of good,
  than all the sages can. —William Wordsworth

DECEMBER 24

- *Hear the other side.* —St. Augustine
- *A useless life is an early death.* —Goethe
- *How small it's all.* —James Joyce
- *We are involved in a life that passes understanding and our highest business is our daily life.* —John Cage
- *About the most originality that any writer can hope to achieve honestly is to steal with good judgement.* —Josh Billings
- *We form a habit of conquering as insistent as any other habit. Victory becomes, to some degree, a state of mind. Knowing ourselves superior to the anxieties, troubles, and worries which obsess us, we are superior to them. It is a question of attitude in confronting them.* —Virginia Hanson

DECEMBER 25

- *By their fruits you shall know them.* —Bible
- *Thou shalt love thy neighbour as thyself.* —Bible
- *Familiar acts are beautiful through love.* —Percy Bysshe Shelley
- *Throw a lucky man in the sea,*
  and he will come up with a fish in his mouth. —Arab Proverb
- *The art of medicine consists of amusing*
  the patient while nature cures the disease. —Voltaire
- *I firmly believe that if the whole material medica as now used,*
  could be sunk to the bottom of the sea, it would be all the better for mankind and all the worse for the fishes. —Holmes

DECEMBER 26

- *Out of their own mouth will I judge thee.* —Bible
- *Thou art more lovely and more temperate.* —Shakespeare
- *Love those who love you.* —Voltaire
- *But, soft! What light through yonder window breaks?*
  It is the east, and Juliet is the sun. —Shakespeare
- *If it walks like a duck and quacks like a duck,*
  then it just may be a duck. —Walter Reuther
- *"Is there any point to which you would*
  wish to draw my attention?"
  "To the curious incident of the dog in the night-time".
  "The dog did nothing in the night-time."
  "That was the curious incident," remarked Sherlock Holmes.
  —A. Conan Doyle

DECEMBER 27

- *Character is destiny.* —Heraclitus
- *Love comforteth like sunshine after rain.* —Shakespeare
- *A pity beyond all telling*
  Is hid in the heart of love. —William Butler Yeats
- *The most savage controversies are about those matters*
  as to which there is no good evidence either way.
  —Bertrand Russell
- *Courage is armor*
  a blind man wears;
  The calloused scar
  of outlived repairs;
  Courage is fear
  that has said its prayers. —Karle W. Baker

DECEMBER 28

- *A thing of beauty is a joy for ever.* —John Keats
- *A lucky man is rarer than a white cow.* —Juvenal
- *The lucky person passes for a genius.* —Euripides
- *Have, but luck, and you will have the rest;*
  be fortunate, and you will be thought great. —Victor Hugo
- *Intellectual rubbish in unpopular essays*
  things seen are mightier than things heard. —Alfred
- *Our youth began with tears and sighs,*
  with seeking what we could not find;
  We sought and knew not what we sought;
  We marvel, now we look behind :
  Life's more amusing than we thought. —Andrew Lang

DECEMBER 29

- *What do you today can improve all your tomorrows.* —Ralph Morston
- *Luck is the residue of design.* —Branch Rickey
- *Luck never made a man wise.* —Seneca
- *Human life is but a series of footnotes to*
  a vast obscure unfinished masterpiece. Vladimir Nabokov
- *You cannot escape the responsibility of tomorrow by evading it today.* —Abraham Lincoln
- *I never saw a wild thing*
  sorry for itself.
  A small bird will drop frozen dead
  from a bough
  without ever having left sorry for itself. —D. H. Lawrence

DECEMBER 30

- *When something is important enough, you do it even if the odd are not in your favour.* —Elon Musk
- *I married beneath me-all women do.* —Nancy Astor
- *Fortune favours the brave.* —Terence
- *For men must work and women must weep,*
  and the sooner it's over, the sooner to sleep. —Charles Kingsley
- *A man lives by believing something, not by debating*
  and arguing about many things. —Thomas Carlyle
- *A wonderful bird is the pelican,*
  his bill will hold more than his belican.
- *He can take in his beak enough food for a week,*
  but I'm darned if I know how the helican. —Dixon Merriti

DECEMBER 31

- *It is by forgiving that one is forgiven.* —Mother Teresa
- *Let there be spaces in your togetherness.* —Kabul Gibran
- *It is better to marry than to burn.* —Bible
- *When we are born, we cry that we are come to this great stage of fools.* —Shakespeare
- *There are no such things as incurables; there are only things for which man has not found a cure.* —Bernard M. Baruch
- *Doctors are men who prescribe medicines of which they know little, to cure diseases of which they know less, in human beings of whom they know nothing.* —Voltaire
- *Books serve to show a man that those original thoughts of his aren't very new after all.* —Abraham Lincoln
- *The spark of life within and without is ever the same. In an atom is the whole Kingdom of God. In one grain are numberless worlds. There is but one principle in soul and body. He who knows this must follow the mystery of nature.* —Ancient Chinese Book
- *Courage is sometimes frail as hope is frail: A fragile shoot between two stones, that grows brave toward the sun though warmth and brightness fail, striving and faith the only strength it knows.* —Frances Rodman

STOP PRESS!